M000013518

What people are saying about …

FIGHT FOR THEIR HEARTS

"Tim and Kenny have a gift for applying the gospel of Jesus to fatherhood. They remind us that if we want to raise kids who are grounded in the gospel, we need to be grounded in the gospel ourselves. This book offers much-needed encouragement, focus, and practical guidance for dads like me who know they don't have everything figured out. Dads, move this book to the top of your reading list."

Dr. Jesse Welliver, LifeGroups Pastor,
Eagle's Landing First Baptist Church

M46 DADS TESTIMONIALS

"M46 Dads provides clear instruction using God's Word to be the father and husband that God intended us to be. You will be challenged with each lesson to ask your children a question that will clearly reveal your relationship with them."

Ben

"I thought I did everything right by my seven kids, but my parenting style created some strains in our relationships. M46 showed me how to love like God, have grace and mercy like God, and place myself in my kids' shoes when they didn't measure up to my standards and expectations."

Shawn

"Each session of M46 Dads gives you a new tool for being a leader and encourager to your children, as well as a new challenge for you as a father and a man in general. I believe men need to congregate to be their strongest, and as iron sharpens iron, M46 will sharpen any man's ability to be the godly father each of us is destined to be."

Matthew

"I am so thankful for M46 Dads, a place that I can go to be equipped to be the type of dad I want to be for my sons. I just wish we could have had something like this many years ago when I was a child. I wish my dad could have been involved in something like this."

Greg

"M46 Dads has changed my life! It lets me be real, with real guys in my group, and has shown me how to be a better husband, father, and follower of Jesus. All the analogies used in this study have opened a line of communication that I've never had with my kids before."

Adam

"M46 Dads has helped me, a young, first time father of a toddler, to establish a firm foundation to build on. It has spoken louder than the world's definition of 'fatherhood' and allowed me to start parenting with the end in mind."

Marcus

"Being the father of two teenagers, I've found M46 Dads extremely helpful in getting meaningful conversations going with my boys. It reminds and humbles me on the importance of being an involved dad. Meeting with like-minded and godly dads is reassuring that we are all in the same battle for the hearts of our children."

Chris

"Having done many Bible studies over the years, I've had a hard time retaining their information. The creators of M46 Dads have taken a new approach! Each week is a new nugget of information that they drive home using visual aids. As I spend time with my kids, I'm now mindful of what it takes to be intentional and what it means to be a good father."

Brandon

"M46 Dads is a group of men who gather, seek God, and share their experiences, strengths, and hopes so they can build better and lasting relationships with their children. M46 Dads is direct, in-your-face biblical teachings that tell us men what our role is as fathers to our children."

Scott

"The Lord took my wife and me along an amazing adoption journey that led us to adopt four beautiful siblings from foster care. I love M46 Dads because it gives me the tools and encouragement I need to make an impact for Christ in the lives of my children."

Matt

"M46 Dads continues to be a place where a community of men who desire to be the priests of their homes get together and learn from each other. The Bible-based instructions I have received have helped me become more intentional in my relationships with my sons. M46 Dads is helping me and other men live in a way that God wants us to live."

Clifton

"With guidance from M46 meetings and materials, I persuaded my son, who previously avoided me, to commit to 30 days of at least 10 minutes of interaction together each day. During that experience, we grew in understanding of each other, our challenges, disappointments, and victories. We now interact on a different level, and he knows I love him and that I'm sincere."

Murrell

"M46 Dads helps me calibrate my 'daddy compass' each month. I'm so thankful for the power of fellowship around God's Word."

Pat

"M46 Dads helps dads who are trying to get it right to not feel alone when they do it wrong. Dads understand why 'the struggle is real' as they learn how to have victory in the most important role of their lives: being Christlike, loving, caring, strong fathers who can equip the next generation for His kingdom."

Mike

"The regular M46 Dads meetings have helped me understand the things of God more, think about how my relationships with my children are related to their relationships with God, and be more intentional with my family in growing in God."

Matt

"I wanted to be a God-first father from day one. The leaders of M46 Dads were as raw and transparent as they come; they would openly describe real-life scenarios where they jacked up and also where they got it right. M46 Dads is a place where men will be equipped to be our best, but it is never a place where you have to act like you are perfect and have it all together."

Bubba

"My children and my children's children will benefit from M46 Dads, and that's what it's all about to me."

Michael

"M46 has given me so much insight, especially when it comes to showing dads the difference between raising sons and daughters. Personally, it has made me a better father, son, and Christian leader within my household."

Greg

"I am not the father I want to be, but M46 helps me believe that I can be!"

Jason

FIGHT
FOR THEIR
HEARTS

FOREWORD BY MARK HALL OF CASTING CROWNS

FIGHT
FOR THEIR
HEARTS

HOPE & HELP FOR EVERY DAD

KENNY DALLAS & TIM SEXTON
with Robert Noland

M-16 DADS

*And he will turn
the hearts of fathers to their children
and the hearts of children to their fathers.*
Malachi 4:6 ESV

DAVID **C** COOK

transforming lives together

FIGHT FOR THEIR HEARTS
Published by David C Cook
4050 Lee Vance Drive
Colorado Springs, CO 80918 U.S.A.

Integrity Music Limited, a Division of David C Cook
Brighton, East Sussex BN1 2RE, England

The graphic circle C logo is a registered trademark of David C Cook.

All rights reserved. Except for brief excerpts for review purposes,
no part of this book may be reproduced or used in any form
without written permission from the publisher.

The website addresses recommended throughout this book are offered as a
resource to you. These websites are not intended in any way to be or imply an
endorsement on the part of David C Cook, nor do we vouch for their content.

Bible credits are listed at the back of the book.

Library of Congress Control Number 2020948433
ISBN 978-0-8307-8129-4
eISBN 978-0-8307-8132-4

© 2021 The M46 Revolution, Inc.

The Team: Michael Covington, Robert Noland, Jeff Gerke,
Megan Stengel, Jack Campbell, Susan Murdock
Cover Design: James Hershberger

Printed in the United States of America
First Edition 2021

1 2 3 4 5 6 7 8 9 10

011521

Dedication

From Kenny

To my wife, Shannon: Asking you to marry me was the best decision I have ever made. From the day I met you in the sixth grade to when we started dating in the eleventh grade, through six kids and twenty-six years of marriage and until now … you truly are a Proverbs 31 woman and my "warrior." I love you with all my heart!

To my children, Jacob, Caleb, Joshua, David, Elly, and Zech: "Like arrows in the hands of a warrior are children born in one's youth. Blessed is the man whose quiver is full of them." My life is truly blessed and full of joy because of each of you. I am so proud to be your dad. I love each of you with all my heart!

From Tim

To my wife, Georgia—my warrior! God placed you in my life to tether me to something solid while I thrashed around trying to grow up. I wasn't ready for you, and I surely wasn't ready to be a dad. But God is good. He has taught us both how to love each other, and He has blessed us beyond measure. You are my best friend and a tangible rock that we all count on every day. I am so thankful that you are the mother of our children. You are true and faithful, and your love for Jesus inspires me. I love you.

To our four boys, Joshua, Jordan, Jesse, and Ezra: I am so thankful for all of you. I am blessed to be your dad, and I love this season of life where I get to watch you all as men. I couldn't be more proud, and you are the greatest legacy a dad could hope for. I love you all.

CONTENTS

Part Two: Family

Part Three: Field

Acknowledgments

To our board of directors: Clifton Youngblood, Robbie Moore, Mike Holmes, Jay Kimsey, Les Lambert, and Mark Hall. Thank you all for your support, encouragement, friendship, and wisdom over the years. None of this would have been possible without you. Each of you is a true man of God and an image-bearer of the one true King!

To the men of Eagle's Landing and Trinity, thank you! Thank you for being a part of our first CRASH communities. Thank you for being real, transparent, and faithful. Thank you for being men who desire to fight for the hearts of your children!

A Foreword from Mark Hall of Casting Crowns

As a man who follows Jesus, there is no role in my life that I take more seriously than being a dad to my own four children. Having been a youth pastor for decades, I am reminded every day of the crucial role we as fathers play in our families. Week in and week out as my team and I minister to students, I see the power of dads both in their presence *and* absence. Traveling the world through the ministry of Casting Crowns is another way I have witnessed the incredible importance of our ministry as men when we choose to be the spiritual leaders, not just providers and protectors, of our homes.

Growing up as I became a man, there were many challenges I had to face. I was so grateful for the people in my life who were there for me when things got dark, when I had someone to go to for help and hope. But as I became a dad, I quickly saw that journey as a man can be one of the loneliest paths we walk. Because we're not really sure what the rules are. We aren't certain where to go when something's not working out with our children. And then when we think we have one kid figured out, our next is totally different, and we start all over.

Too often, we just feel like we are totally blowing this fatherhood thing. I remember thinking that it would be so good if someone, anyone, could come alongside and run a few laps with me, to let me know that other dads feel like I did, like they're blowing it too. *But* also that we can go to God together to find encouragement and strength to grow and press on.

I want you to know that M46 Dads has become that community *for me*. And I'm so grateful and excited to let you know that M46 is now available *for you*.

When I first experienced M46 Dads at our church, Eagle's Landing, and the work that Tim and Kenny were doing together, the first thing I loved was their approach. A CRASH meeting felt more like circling up at a campfire than attending a church service. No one came off like an expert telling the rest of us what we needed to change. There was zero condemnation, only grace.

M46 started as a room full of dads coming together to admit to God and each other that we needed help. Our meetings were just guys who loved Jesus and our families trying to be real, to be honest, and to encourage each other, to walk together in getting better at one of the toughest jobs on the planet these days—being a dad. Guys who have each other's backs to take on the biggest opportunity we will ever have—to truly be warriors in fighting for the hearts of our kids.

In my role as a youth pastor, I talk to a lot of dads about the things they struggle with as fathers and how they parent. What I hear a lot today is *fear*. Dads are scared about what is going to happen to their kids. Or afraid their kids are going to do the same things they did. Or their kids are going to get mixed up in some tragic situation. But our parenting, especially in this culture, has got to come from a walk with Jesus, from the truth that He's making us new day by day, and He is doing the same thing for our kids. We have to let Jesus give us a new battle cry to lead our families.

Lastly, I want to be straight with you about Tim and Kenny's content in this book. This is not a "top ten tips to become a better father" book. It does not come with a "just do these things and your kids will turn out great" guarantee. This is *not* a behavior-modification manual. This is a road map written by fellow strugglers that can lead you, Dad, to the Father's heart. To be certain you understand and grasp the love, mercy, and grace of God. That you can know the best Source in heaven and on earth to find the hope and help you need to be the man God designed you to be for *your kids*. For you to literally experience the Lord turn your heart to your children and your children's hearts to you.

So let's do this. Let's dive in *together* and become M46 Dads!

A Word from Kenny and Tim before You Begin

We want to assure you that we are not parenting experts. Every single word we teach and write is meant for *us* first. We share these chapters with you after years of experience as dads, as well as many years in ministry. Between us, we have ten kids at home, so we've had lots of learning the hard way.

When I (Kenny) speak at our CRASH meetings and other men's rallies, I always say, "If any of you think I have this parenting thing figured out and perfected, just come visit my house on some random night and you can see the truth for yourselves." I can assure you that Tim and I are fellow strugglers in fatherhood.

At our M46 Dads meetings, which we call "CRASHes," we work hard to create an atmosphere where men don't feel the need to pretend they've got being a dad figured out. We are just a group of guys who want to honor the Lord, love our kids the way He wants us to, and become better equipped to be the dads our children deserve.

In our ministry, we are all about two key elements:

1. We believe Scripture calls men to be the primary spiritual leaders of their homes.

2. We want to help equip *you* to be that spiritual leader in *your* home.

Many great truths in Scripture, when properly understood, can be applied as principles to guide us as dads. Our goal in each chapter of this book is to offer you a *guiding principle*, provide you with a *specific challenge* to be intentional, and encourage you to *be intentional* with your kids.

Chapters 1 and 2 will lay the foundation for the rest of the book to answer *why* you should accept the challenge to become an M46 Dad.

Part 1 contains chapters 3 through 5, which dive into our relationship with God and how we can best communicate Him to our children.

Part 2 contains chapters 6 through 8, which focus on our relationships with our families and loved ones, as well as how to be the fathers our children deserve.

Part 3 contains chapters 9 and 10, which challenge us in our impact on others and how that can involve our own children.

The M46 Dads Challenge at the end of each chapter is a simple and practical application for you to do with your children. Applying the principle will connect the truth to your own life and parenting. These challenges can also establish new spiritual interactions with your kids.

Also at the end of each chapter is an M46 Moment. These are brief testimonies from fathers who saw the truth and promise of Malachi 4:6 happen in their own lives. Each story is about *the moment* when the heart of the father was turned toward his children and the gospel began to redeem, transform, and make things new. We hope these stories—from dads just like you—will offer great inspiration and encouragement in your relationship with your children.

We are asking you to commit to completing this entire book. Finish every chapter and complete every challenge. As you read, you will be guided as a father and challenged to be intentional and take action with your children.

Chapter 1

Painting the Picture

As Christ-followers, we all have a story that shapes us for good or bad. But the common denominator in them all is that the gospel has truly set us free. In fact, the gospel is the *only* force that can set men free.

That is not some super-spiritual Christianese cliché but the reality of our lives. We have been radically transformed by the power of Christ. Outside of Jesus' intervention, there is no explanation for our lives. He said, "For apart from me you can do nothing" (John 15:5). We know that. We believe that. We live it every day.

I (Tim) have four sons, two daughters-in-law, a granddaughter, and a grandson.

I (Kenny) have five sons and one daughter.

For better or worse, we had fathers who impacted our own lives. In our individual journeys, we have each been shaped and influenced by our fathers, just as you have. And now, as dads ourselves, we are shaping and influencing the next generation through our own children.

Whether a father is present or absent, encouraging or condemning, motivating or paralyzing, he has a powerful effect on his children. Deeply mindful of that fact, we started M46 Dads because we saw a massive need. We also realized a huge gap in our little corner of the ministry world. Our hearts are to help our brothers be the best dads they can be. That is the sole mission of M46 Dads.

While we each have very different stories, the gospel can and must transform us from the inside out. The gospel exists because of, and for, our failures. That's the point.

That's why we have included our own stories in this book. We want you to see in our lives the enormous influence that fathers have on the lives of their children. Of course dads impact their kids, but what we have discovered is that many are not *intentional* about their influence in the lives of their children.

What's more, many dads simply don't realize the massive wounds they may leave in the hearts of their kids. A father's influence is far greater than most of us know. And all too often, when we finally do understand, damage may be done and a great deal of hurt must be worked through in the relationship.

Whether a father works hard to positively impact his children or he vanishes, leaving no physical presence in their lives, he will make an immeasurable impact. Your own father influenced you, for better or worse. In the same way, you will influence your children, for better or worse.

You didn't have a choice about what your dad did with you. But you have *your own choice now.*

THE PAINTBRUSH

Imagine a father holding a paintbrush in his hand, painting a picture of God for his children. A dad can paint a beautiful and accurate picture of the Father, and his children will have an easier time seeing

God for who He truly is as they grow up. They will see a God of grace who disciplines out of love for the good of His children. They will see a God who is engaged in who they are and who is focused on their hearts.

Or a dad can paint a broken and twisted image of God for his children to see. In some cases, this picture can be so wrong that they are forced to spend their lifetimes trying to erase that picture. They will see an angry God, a distant God, or a God who is indifferent, unavailable, and uncaring.

As a father, you *will* create and shape your children's concept of God. What an awesome but terrible prospect to consider. You can try to put the paintbrush down and run away, but the minute you became a father, that brush was permanently attached. Even if you're not physically or emotionally present, your absence still paints a picture. That's simply part of the deal in being a dad.

The wonderful thing about the gospel—the person of Jesus—is that He can take the mistakes, the faulty brushstrokes we're responsible for, and still create a beautiful picture with what we give Him. But that happens only when we surrender the brush and invite Him to guide our painting.

THE M46 MISSION

The mission of M46 Dads is to inspire and equip fathers to fight for the hearts of their children. That brings us to the meaning of our name. *M46* is a reference to the very last Bible verse in the Old Testament: "And he will turn the hearts of fathers to their children and the hearts of children to their fathers" (Mal. 4:6 ESV).

The mission of M46 Dads is to inspire and equip fathers to fight for the hearts of their children.

This verse holds a great truth and also an amazing promise to all of us as both men and fathers. However, a little explanation is needed to fully understand the context.

While the *he* in this verse seems to refer to the prophet Elijah, many theologians believe it is a specific reference to John the Baptist. Luke 1:17 states, "He will go before him in the spirit and power of Elijah, to turn the hearts of the fathers to the children" (ESV). God anointed John the Baptist as the one to prepare the hearts of the people for Jesus.

In Malachi 4:6, we are told that one of the results of the gospel would be to "turn the hearts of fathers to their children, and the hearts of children to their fathers." In Luke 1:17, we begin to see this promise fulfilled in Christ.

The powerful truth of Malachi 4:6 is that the heart of God desires to see dads and their children drawn toward, not away from, one another. The promise is that as a man's heart is turned toward God and he begins to truly understand the fierce, unconditional love and the powerful redemptive grace of the gospel, his heart will naturally turn toward his children. Every man—throughout all generations—needs this truth and promise from the Father's heart for his family.

The essential truth every man must understand is that, regardless of your situation, God is with you as you fight for the hearts of your children. Malachi 4:6 communicates love, blessing, favor, hope, redemption, unity, and legacy. And God offers all of these to us as His sons.

Regardless of your situation, God is with you as you fight for the hearts of your children.

M46 Dads is about helping those fathers who have done a great job and those fathers who have rarely gotten it right. Through this boots-on-the-ground ministry, we have seen God do extraordinary things through ordinary dads just like us. Our heavenly Father is good, always restoring and reconciling, when we submit and surrender to Him.

As two fathers who love Jesus and want to influence our children to love Him too, we have a strong desire to help other dads engage with their kids through their journeys. We want to help the next generation see God for who He truly is and then also get a clear and accurate picture of the gospel.

While you are painting that picture for your kids, God can do a mighty work. He can heal, mend, and transform. He gave you the

awesome ability and intimidating responsibility to communicate to
your children what He is like.

Let's pray.

*"Heavenly Father, we pray for our new friend who is reading this
book right now. We ask that You take him from wherever he is, in whatever position he finds himself, with anything he has or hasn't done, and
begin to show him Your vision and heart for himself and his children.
Restore what must be restored. Heal what needs to be healed. Redeem
what has to be redeemed. Help his heart turn to You first and then to his
children to paint the picture You desire to be displayed of You and Your
love. In Jesus' name, amen."*

M46 Dads Challenge One

Describe the picture of God that your father painted for you.

Describe the picture of God that you are currently painting for your kids.

How are you painting differently from how your own father painted for you?

Where are the hearts of your children turned today?

Fight for the hearts of your children!

Kenny's Story

The Blessing in Brokenness

My father is my mentor. He is my sacred counselor. He is a trusted friend. There is no one I love and respect more than him. But that has not always been true. In fact, for many years, our relationship was very much the opposite. Here's my story.

My parents got married right out of high school, and soon after, I was born. They were just two kids with a kid.

When my dad was twenty-one and my mom was twenty, not long after my brother was born, they got a divorce.

I grew up living with my mom, and both she and my dad eventually remarried other people. They each had two more children, giving my brother and me four sisters with whom I became very close. Over time, Mom and Dad created new lives about an hour apart from each other.

My mom always made sure I was in a good school district where I could play baseball and football. I've always loved sports, playing a lot of Wiffle ball and pickup basketball games in the neighborhood after school and on weekends.

I had tremendous role models in my life—amazing grand-parents, coaches, and teachers. But the single greatest influence I wanted and needed most was the very one I had the least amount of time with—my dad.

Because of my father having a second family an hour away, and due to his busy work schedule, I rarely saw him. Once a month or so, my brother and I would spend the weekend at his house. I was always struck by what a great athlete Dad was when we played any kind of ball together. He was also a great storyteller. I recall that as a young child I didn't feel angry as much as sad about his absence, because I couldn't spend more time with this man who I thought was so incredible.

As a kid, I had no way of understanding how hard it must have been on my dad living an hour away from me and my brother or how tough it must have been on him to work the graveyard shift at the plant where he was employed. As a little boy growing up, all I knew was that I really missed my dad. There was always this ache of sadness in my gut that I couldn't escape.

While I rarely talked about how I felt, those feelings were always there. I missed him being at my games, school events, and in the little moments of everyday life.

Over the years, the desire to spend time with my dad never went away, and other things were slowly added to my sadness: bitterness and resentment. And those two feelings, left to fester in your heart, can poison you.

MY M46 MOMENT

The summer after I graduated high school, something happened that changed everything. Along with my girlfriend, Shannon, who later became my wife, I attended a Fourth of July celebration at a church. Little did I know that this Independence Day was about to have a special significance for my personal freedom.

Although I had grown up with my mom taking me to church, at this event I encountered the gospel in a powerful way, as if it were the first time I had ever heard the message. I completely surrendered my life to Jesus. I remember the pastor appealing for anyone who wanted to accept Christ, be baptized, or surrender to ministry. I raised my hand to them *all*. I was in!

As a new believer, I began to study the Bible; then one day, I came across where Jesus said, "Forgive us our sins, as we have forgiven those who sin against us" (Matt. 6:12). The notes at the bottom of the page in my study Bible said that Jesus was communicating that God will forgive our sins in the same manner that we forgive others.

In that moment, I knew I had to forgive my dad and get rid of the deep bitterness and resentment built up in my heart for his absence in my life.

Later, in my last year of college, I saw that the Promise Keepers men's movement had an event scheduled in Memphis at the Liberty Bowl. I asked my dad if he would go with me. He agreed.

As soon as the first speaker finished his presentation, which was about the power of the gospel, my father turned to me and said we needed to talk. With tears in his eyes, he told me he knew that he wasn't around much as I grew up, and he asked me if I would forgive him.

I don't know exactly what had happened to cause my dad to open up and ask for my forgiveness, but in that moment, my heart was turned toward my father. I absolutely and completely forgave him.

It wasn't until many years later that I discovered Malachi 4:6. And I saw then that this verse is actually a promise of what happens through the gospel—and it was *exactly* what had happened with my dad and me.

In that divine appointment with my father, God completely redeemed a broken relationship that had been filled with sadness, loneliness, bitterness, and resentment. Our heavenly Father began to lead us together down a path to a new relationship in which, over time, my dad would become my mentor and trusted counselor. Today, he is the man I look up to more than anyone else in this world. Jesus Christ can and does redeem and make "all things new" (Rev. 21:5 ESV).

WHEN THE STORM HITS

My relationships with God and my dad were firmly in place and growing stronger every day. After marrying my high school sweetheart, Shannon, and graduating from college, I became a high school football coach.

You'll recall that, in my response to the pastor's altar call, I had also raised my hand to surrender to the ministry. In college, I had originally been a religion major, even considering going to seminary. I remember telling Shannon that on top of majoring in religion, I was also going to add physical education/health. She responded, "Instead of seminary, you're going to be a gym teacher?"

But it did not take long to realize that my true calling and desire were to challenge and inspire young men to become all God had created them to be. How better to reach out and influence the lives of young men than to be a high school football coach? Coaching football became our ministry and remains so to this day.

Over the years, Shan and I had six beautiful children. I always made just enough money for her to be a stay-at-home mom, which was her dream. In my coaching career, we have had a lot of success building a championship football program, and I have also been blessed to carry out my personal calling to young men.

In Matthew 7, we find Jesus' parable of the house built on rock and the house built on sand. Each house faced a storm of driving wind and rain. When I was thirty-nine years old, *my* storm hit.

I had just finished my sixteenth year of coaching high school football. My team had played for the state championship in the Georgia Dome in Atlanta, and I had been named the Associated Press Coach of the Year for the state of Georgia. My wife loved me, and she was happy living her dream as a wife and mom with our six healthy children.

Though I had the world by the tail, for reasons I could see only later, I was extremely restless, and this made me start to think it was time to make a change.

I received an offer to help lead a relatively new school as an administrator, which would be a completely different role for me and in another state. This change would mean uprooting my happy family and rocking their world. But, convinced the move was God's will, I announced to my family, team, school, and church that I was taking the job.

To this day, explaining exactly what happened is very hard for me. The city where we went was fantastic and so were the people. But even before the move, something happened inside my heart. I quickly began to question myself and became deeply concerned that I had made a huge mistake and was not a fit for the job at all.

My family had placed all their trust in me. The staff at the new job was counting on me to come and be a leader. For the first time in my life, I did not know what to do. I started to experience anxiety like never before. I was terrified of failure and of letting everyone down. To make matters worse, I was feeling a deep sense of embarrassment and shame because I had stood up in front of everyone I knew and confidently proclaimed, "This is God's will for my life."

All my life, I had always been Mr. Optimistic. My glass was not just half-full but usually running over. I always found the positives and possibilities in everything. But in this situation, I was struggling like I never had before. I began to mercilessly second-guess myself, constantly thinking, *What have I done? How could I have uprooted my entire family? Am I an idiot? Do I even know how to hear God's voice? Am I running away from something? Am I a coward and afraid to face this?* The questions played on repeat in my mind.

I never imagined that I of all people would have experienced these feelings while standing on the doorstep of turning forty years old, but I was quickly spiraling downward into depression. I felt like I had fallen into a deep pit and had no idea how to crawl out. Fear, anxiety, and doubt became an everyday part of my life.

For sixteen years as a football coach, I'd had to make all my decisions with a twenty-five-second play clock counting down. But now, I was experiencing "paralysis by analysis." I didn't just feel like a total failure—I *knew* I was a failure! As much as I tried to keep my secret from those around me, there was no hiding from God and my own heart.

I wish I could say that I turned to Scripture for answers, but I didn't. I wish I could say that I reached out to a group of Christian brothers for help, but I didn't. I wish I could say that I worshipped my way out of the struggle, but that would not be true. I became more and more isolated, even from my family.

My inner battle began to have a stronger and stronger hold on me. Everything in my life suffered, especially my relationship with my wife and kids. To make the move work, I had even taken a cut in salary with the promise that the pay would increase over the first few years. The home we'd left in Atlanta had not sold, so we had two house payments and two sets of utility bills—on decreased pay. We fell behind on our mortgage and eventually lost the previous home to foreclosure. My wife gave up her dream of being at home and went back to work as a nurse.

So many thoughts raced through my mind. I knew we could not stay where we were, but leaving would hurt some very good people. The thought of admitting to the folks back home that I had missed God was devastating. All this on top of losing the house made my sense of failure overwhelming. As a pull-yourself-up-by-your-own-bootstraps guy, I was now broken, weak, and filled with guilt and shame.

LIFT YOUR HEAD AND RISE UP

One day, on the brink of a complete breakdown, I took a long walk into the woods. I knew I had to get completely alone with God. Hidden among the trees, I sat down and prayed as honestly as I could. I told the Lord that I felt I was at the bottom of a pit. I confessed my innermost fears and that I had no idea what to do. I poured out my heart and soul to God.

Honestly, I had not had a "quiet time" or read God's Word in a while. Strange how our worst seasons in life can often keep us away from the very things that can bring real answers. Though I have never heard God's audible voice, as I sat completely broken before the Lord, in my spirit I heard these whispered words: "Though a just man falls seven times, he rises again," which is a paraphrase of the first part of Proverbs 24:16.

In that moment, God became the "lifter of my head" that Psalm 3:3 (ESV) talks about. I had never understood that verse from King David until that day. I felt as if God physically lifted my head from looking down to looking up. For the first time in a very long while, I heard a word from the Lord for *me*: "Lift your head and rise up!" In a heartbeat, I was filled with a tremendous sense of God's purpose. At the bottom of the pit, and at the end of myself, my heavenly Father was there.

At the bottom of the pit, and at the end of myself, my heavenly Father was there.

I can never escape from your Spirit!
 I can never get away from your presence!
If I go up to heaven, you are there;
 if I go down to the grave, you are there.
If I ride the wings of the morning,
 if I dwell by the farthest oceans,
even there your hand will guide me,
 and your strength will support me.

I could ask the darkness to hide me
     and the light around me to become night—
     but even in darkness I cannot hide from you.
To you the night shines as bright as day.
          (Ps. 139:7–12)

I hurried home and told Shannon exactly what had happened in the woods. With a sense of new life and excitement running through my spirit, I said that I knew two things: God was not done with me, and I was supposed to "rise up."

Shan looked me in the eyes and asked, "So, Kenny Dallas, you feel like you are a failure?"

I nodded. "Yes, I do."

"We have six children," she said. "How many of them do you think are going to fail at something? A business? A marriage? Anything?"

Not knowing where she was going, I responded, "All of them will at some point."

Then my wife delivered her final shot: "Well, then ... show them how to do it!"

Later, Shan told me that she had said the same thing to me at least a dozen times before. But for whatever reason, *that* was the first time I ever remembered hearing her say the words. I heard her clearly that day, and I knew the challenge was for me as a dad.

During this tough season, some wonderful people supported and encouraged me. I appreciated everyone, but two people knew *all* the ugly details and yet still walked alongside me through it all. First was Shannon. The Hebrew word for "help mate" (see Gen. 2:18) also conveys the idea of being a husband's warrior. She has always fought for me and is most certainly my warrior.

The other person who walked with me through it all was my dad. He called me, prayed for me and with me, listened to me, came to see me, and even helped us financially. The absolute toughest time of my life hit when I was thirty-nine years old. And my dad was there for me!

During that really difficult season, I knew I had fully surrendered my heart to the Lord. I knew I loved my family. Going back to Jesus' analogy about the two houses, I felt that mine was "falling with a mighty crash." But our home was built on Christ the Rock, so while the house shook, we stood and even rose up, just like He promised would happen.

STRENGTHEN YOUR BROTHERS

As I began to look back and evaluate, I realized I had some serious issues with my identity. My worth as a man had been defined by how many games I'd won as a coach and by my reputation in the world's eyes. I came to understand that my value must be found solely in Christ and His finished work on the cross.

I also learned that a leader cannot become an island. A man needs others with whom he can be transparent, be honest, and walk alongside. My wife, my family, my teams, and this world do not need me to put up a front of strength. They deserve a husband, daddy, and leader who knows his strength comes from Christ alone.

Today, all these years later, I have the opportunity to tell my story of brokenness to men. I love to show how, even at the bottom of the pit, you can find your heavenly Father. But I also get to tell them my personal M46 Moment about Christ redeeming my relationship with my dad and how, as a grown man, when I needed him the most, he was right there with me.

I did move my family back to the Atlanta area. We started attending Eagle's Landing Church. A huge blessing coming out of my season of failure was meeting Tim Sexton, who would become my partner in ministry and coauthor.

The time had come for me to move on from past regrets and press on to whatever the Lord had for our family. In my reset, I was encouraged by Philippians 3:13–14: "Forgetting what is behind and straining toward what is ahead, I press on toward the goal to win the prize for which God has called me" (NIV).

I had a renewed desire to once again coach and challenge young men. But I also had a new passion to provide a place where dads could go to be inspired and equipped as leaders of their homes. In my season of struggle, I had desperately needed inspiration, so I wanted to provide that ministry to other men.

When I met Tim and heard him explain the gospel in the powerful and transparent way he speaks, I knew immediately he was a man I wanted as a friend.

As Tim and I formed the early stages of Operation M46—now M46 Dads—we knew we wanted men to have a place to go and be transparent, because this fatherhood thing is hard. We both knew this needed to be more like an AA meeting than a church service. We wanted to create a space for men like us to say, "Hi, my name is Kenny Dallas. I love my kids and I want to honor the Lord, but I really need some help!"

From day one, Tim and I saw M46 as a ministry that is driven from a place of weakness and brokenness rather than as we-have-all-the-answers parenting gurus. This ministry is truly about surrendering and trusting Jesus to help us be the best dads we can be for our kids.

Just before they went to the Garden of Gethsemane, Jesus said to Peter: "But I have prayed for you, Simon, that your faith may not fail. And when you have turned back, strengthen your brothers" (Luke 22:32 NIV).

Jesus knew that Peter was about to suffer the biggest failure of his life. And yet He told him to lift his head, rise up, and help his brothers. What an incredible picture of the power of grace in the gospel. Jesus wasn't freaked out about Peter's failure. He knew failure would be part of his journey to ready him to "strengthen your brothers."

Tim and I see our ministry to dads as simply helping men step away from the fear and feelings of failure to come to a place of strength and confidence in Christ.

Out of my very difficult season, Shannon's constant prayer was, "God, please redeem every ounce of pain and use it for Your glory." I believe M46 Dads is the answer to her prayer. At every gathering, men share not only their stories of success but also their stories of failure—past and present. We offer a place where men can come and be honest about their fears and struggles as fathers. There is never a "just suck it up" or "man up" mantra from our camp. The key in redeeming failure is learning that brokenness can bring absolute surrender that leads to true freedom.

Second Corinthians 12:9 states, "'My grace is sufficient for you, for my power is made perfect in weakness.' Therefore I will boast all the more gladly about my weaknesses, so that Christ's power may rest on me" (NIV). Hearing men at every meeting recognize their "weaknesses" in being the dads they want to be is so humbling. And seeing "Christ's power rest on them" when they surrender is always amazing.

Today, with our six beautiful kids, and with the boys I coach and the dads I interact with, I am no longer trying to just teach them how to win. I'm also showing them how to fail. We are blessed to be back to our ministry of challenging young men through serving as the head football coach as well as the director of Student Leadership at Trinity Christian School in Sharpsburg, Georgia. And I now have the profound honor of "strengthening the brothers" each month at our M46 CRASHes, where we inspire and equip fathers to fight for the hearts of their children.

Chapter 2

Starting at the Finish Line

The men's semifinals of the 400-meter race at the 1992 Barcelona Olympics brought everyone to the edge of their seats to see some of the fastest runners on the planet compete. But the world was about to witness one of the most inspiring moments in sports history. Not from the man who won first place, but rather from the one who finished last.

Just by making it to the semifinals, British athlete Derek Redmond proved he was one of the fastest men in the world. He had won his preliminary heat with the best time, so of course he was one of the favorites to win the medal. When the race began, with all the runners in their staggered starting positions, Derek quickly sped forward, seeming to be in prime position to lead the pack when they got to the final straightaway.

Then tragedy struck: Derek's hamstring tore and he collapsed onto the track in pain.

The other runners flew past Derek on their way to Olympic glory, while he knelt on the ground in agony mixed with disbelief.

But rather than being carted off the track, he fought his way back up to his feet and began to hobble along in his lane. His hopes of a medal were gone. Now, he only wanted to cross the finish line. With every step Derek took, the piercing pain in his leg was displayed by the grimacing look on his face as he limped and hopped forward.

Suddenly a man pushed his way through the crowd from the stands, past security personnel and onto the track. Though most people watching in the stadium or on TV couldn't know, this was Derek's dad, Jim Redmond. Jim ran to his son, only wanting to keep him from causing more damage and pain.

But Derek looked over to his father and told him he had to finish the race. So Jim agreed. "Well then, we're going to finish this together." And that is exactly what they did.

With each step he took, the pain grew unbearable, so Derek leaned more on his father like a crutch. Security personnel approached them, but Jim waved them away. They finished the race arm in arm—together, father and son—as the crowd gave a thunderous standing ovation. Never has a last place finish been so inspiring.

This story is powerful, but not because the athletes were so fast. Who can even name the winner of the 400-meter gold medal in the 1992 Olympics? What makes this story so moving is Jim Redmond's intentional love for his boy. He took action to help his hurting son reach his goal and cross the finish line.

So, Dad, let's turn the tables now. Why have *you* taken action to open up this book?

If you're like most men, you have little to no free time. And if you do, you would likely rather look at a screen than read a book. We also assume, again like most of us, that you don't feel perfectly equipped or prepared to be the father you want to be.

But the good news is that *you* have taken action by starting this book.

We're guessing that means you deeply love your kids and want to be the best father you can possibly be ... and that you've realized this fatherhood thing is hard. You've reached for this book because, just like us, you could use some help.

If that is true, then we want you to know you're in good company right now. Barna Research revealed that 89 percent of parents today say they do not feel adequate in training their children. Studies consistently show that the vast majority of fathers in this generation feel they are failing in some area and do not feel equipped to be the type of father they desire to be.[1]

GAME-CHANGING QUESTION

I (Kenny) am about to ask you what is possibly the most important question you've ever been asked, a question my father taught me to ask myself.

Fast-forward to your very last day on earth. Imagine you are very old and lying on your deathbed. You know you are about to pass from this life and stand before the Lord. In that moment ...

What matters?

Take a minute, take a deep breath, close your eyes, and honestly consider that question. What is your answer?

I have asked that question to many men over the years. Answers I have heard include:

- "That I have a genuine relationship with the Lord."
- "That I loved my wife and children well."

- "That I made a difference in the world."
- "That I told others about Jesus."
- "That I spent time with my family and they knew I loved them."
- "That I provided for my family and they are taken care of."
- "That my life mattered."

The list goes on, but the pattern is clear.

What is so interesting about these answers is that they can all be put inside three categories:

1. Relationship with God
2. Relationship with family
3. Relationship with others

Number one has to do with where you stand with the Lord. Numbers two and three have to do with your impact on your circles of influence. Your specific answer may have been worded differently, but I've yet to hear one that doesn't fall within one of these three aspects of life.

I like to define them this way:

- FATHER—Your relationship with God the Father
- FAMILY—Your relationships with your wife and children
- FIELD—Your impact on others in your circles of influence

Dad, by answering this question, do you know what you have just defined? You have defined your finish line.

If you were about to run a race and someone yelled, "On your mark, get set, go!" which way would you run? What direction would you go? You might be able to run fast. You might be able to run hard. But unless you know where your finish line is, you can never have confidence that you are running in the right direction.

Now, let's turn to the other side of our question: On your deathbed in the final moments of this life, what will *not* matter to you? What will you *not* think about? The type of car you drove? The size of your house? How much money you made? Wishing you had spent a few more hours at work?

We all know that money is vital to live. But really, for most men, the only way money will matter in those last moments will be in terms of taking care of loved ones or providing for the great causes we believe in. Even money has value only in terms of relationships inside Father, Family, and Field.

By imagining ourselves on our deathbeds and removing the illusion that we will absolutely still be here tomorrow, we can see with eternal perspective. We can see the difference between what truly matters and what does not.

THE GIFT OF TODAY

Dad, on average, each of us has approximately 6,570 days with our kids from birth through high school graduation. For example, if you currently have a fifteen-year-old, that means you have about one thousand days left before he or she leaves for college or starts a career. You may feel like your kids will be in your home forever, but the reality is that they will be there for only a short season in your life. There is an old saying that goes, "The days are long, but the years are short."

Can you imagine the impact for your children if their father's life was guided by the principle of a godly perspective? What if they had a father who lived with a passionate urgency and was focused on what truly matters? What if his walk with God (Father), his relationship with those closest to him (Family), and his impact on others (Field) were his full focus and priority?

We can get so easily distracted and begin to pursue things that entertain, make us feel good, or feed our flesh, but those will not matter on that last day. Several times in Scripture we see the warning to not turn or look to the left or the right but to keep our eyes fixed on the goal. Why would God tell us not to look around but to focus straight ahead? Because there are so many enticing things that can distract us.

None of us wants to live a life of regret. We don't want to get to the end of our days and wish we had lived differently. The cold, hard fact is that whatever mistakes we have made in the past have real consequences—but with God's grace, they do not have to define our future. We cannot change yesterday, and we're not promised tomorrow, but He has given each of us the precious gift of *today*.

Drink in the absolute wisdom of Psalm 90:12: "Teach us to number our days, that we may gain a heart of wisdom" (NIV).

A heart of wisdom says that if our relationship with Father, Family, and Field is what truly matters on the *last* day, then that is what truly matters on *this* day.

A heart of wisdom says that if our relationship with Father, Family, and Field is what truly matters on the *last* day, then that is what truly matters on *this* day.

THE RHINO REVOLUTION

A revolution may be defined as "an overthrow of a current social order."[2] To be very open and honest with you, we are praying and believing that M46 will absolutely ignite a revolution among dads—in you, your family, your entire community, and your world.

The current social order today includes fatherless homes, of course. But there are also many homes where a man is present yet has no vision for his family.

The problem is not that Christian men don't want to be the spiritual leaders of their homes but that they are simply not equipped to do the job. The right tools are not in our toolboxes, so how can we build what we need? Especially if we haven't had the right things built in us? Regardless, we cannot give what we do not have.

The cover of this book and our ministry logo have the image of a rhino. You might be asking, "What the heck does a rhino have to do with fatherhood?" *Good question.* We chose this animal for three very specific reasons:

First, rhinos are massive beasts that have a distinct and definite presence in their domain. Rhinos can grow to be thirteen feet long and weigh over five thousand pounds.[3] Whether you perceive yourself as a good dad or a bad dad, and no matter your personal circumstances, you are a massive influence with a distinct and definite presence in the lives of your children.

You wouldn't walk into a rhino's enclosure and underestimate him, so do not allow your influence as a father to be underestimated by anyone. But most especially by you! Regardless of how you may feel, your presence in your children's lives is rhino-sized. Just as your father most definitely impacted your life for good or bad, so you impact your kids with the same level of influence.

Second, rhinos can run up to thirty miles per hour but cannot see something until it comes very close.[4] Imagine a rhino charging at full speed—five thousand pounds at thirty miles per hour. But he can see only what's right in front of him. The need for that massive horn and thick skin to protect him becomes easy to understand. As dads who are imperfect, we often struggle to see clearly. We allow our own issues to get in our way, and we crash into things. So, like the rhino, if we are going to run, we are going to have to run by faith, not by sight (2 Cor. 5:7).

Third, rhinos run together in a group called a "crash."[5] Birds fly in flocks. Fish swim in schools. Cattle roam in herds. Rhinos stick together in a crash. (For dads, how can we beat *that* name for our tribe, right?)

From day one at M46 Dads, we have called our gatherings "CRASHes" to remind us of our need for the same strength and unity as a group of rhinos would provide. In a CRASH, we talk openly about our struggles, issues, and challenges as well as our successes and failures. A CRASH is an authentic brotherhood of men who connect to equip one another to become more effective fathers.

Dad, we are rhinos! We are a huge presence in the lives of our children. We will make mistakes in our journeys, so we are going to have to run by faith and not by sight. The great news is that we don't have to run our race alone—we travel alongside other rhinos in our CRASH. Together, we ignite a revolution in our families, our communities, and our world!

READY TO RUN WITH US?

Who is the greatest influence on your children and your family? You! What if the next Great Awakening or revival of God's people happened not in church buildings but in living rooms just like yours all across this nation? Dad, it's time to intentionally take action and fight for the hearts of your children!

What if the next Great Awakening or revival of God's people happened not in church buildings but in living rooms just like yours all across this nation?

As dads, we are in a race. But we are also preparing our children to run their own races. Just like us, they will not run perfectly. Our goal is to inspire and equip you so you are prepared to come alongside your children, put your arms around them, and just like Jim Redmond said, "we're going to finish this together."

Dad, you know your finish line. You know what will matter to you on your deathbed. You know you must run by faith and not by sight. You know now you are a part of a CRASH. And we are running with you.

On your mark, get set, let's go!

M46 Dads Challenge Two

Dad, you are the most influential man in your child's life. This chapter was about a simple question regarding the end of your life: What really matters? Chances are, your answers fell into one or more of these categories:

- Father
- Family
- Field

On a piece of paper or in a journal, write down those three words, leaving plenty of space to write. Under each of those three words, list out three things:

1. A specific goal you want to accomplish
2. Any obstacle standing in your way
3. A scripture—God's truth—that encourages and supports you in overcoming the obstacle to arrive at your goal

For example, let's say that under "Father" you write the goal to "have a closer relationship with God," yet your obstacle is "I struggle to believe He has forgiven my sin." In that case, you need to find a Bible passage—such as "He is so rich in kindness and grace that he purchased our freedom with the blood of his Son and forgave our sins. He has showered his kindness on us, along with all wisdom and understanding" (Eph. 1:7–8)—that will help you get over that obstacle and reach your goal.

Use your Bible, a website (like biblegateway.com), or a Bible app (like YouVersion) to help you. Google searches work great too. Just type "Bible" plus any keywords you're looking for to find a variety of verses to choose from.

Write down at least one goal, one obstacle, and one truth for each of the three *F*s on your sheet. Then begin working on your list toward obedience and answers as you apply God's truth.

If you are part of a CRASH community, bring your page with you to the next meeting (or take a picture of it on your phone for reference). Be ready to share and discuss with your Christian brothers.

Whether you have always known today's truth or you just needed to be reminded and refreshed, or even if you now understand it for the first time, press on and run toward your life's finish line! Now is the time to intentionally take action.

Fight for the hearts of your children!

Tim's Story

Heart of the Child, Heart of the Father

My father was my hero. There is no question that my father was the single greatest influence in my life. Yet I barely knew him. His paintbrush was affected by circumstances outside of his control, which fashioned the picture of God he painted for me.

DAD'S WOUNDS

As a pilot in World War II, my dad participated in battles while aboard the USS *Yorktown*, which was sunk by the Japanese at Midway. He was wounded during the Battle of the Coral Sea; he was scrambling up a ladder to the flight deck when a torpedo struck the ship just below the waterline, right under his feet. He had at least fifty small pieces of shrapnel embedded in his back.

My father's wounds were not significant enough for him to be taken off the ship, so he remained in the sick bay on board. The *Yorktown* was then towed back to Pearl Harbor, where the damage was assessed.

The now-famous Midway decoders had broken the secret code the Japanese used to communicate. And Admiral Chester Nimitz ordered the *Yorktown* to be hastily patched up and sent to rendezvous with the American forces steaming full speed toward Midway to stop the Japanese from taking the island.

The Battle of Midway began when scout planes from the US carriers spotted a lone enemy ship. They then followed the vessel and discovered the location of the entire Japanese fleet.

The Americans caught the Japanese by surprise, and the rest is history—mixed with some legend. But during the course of the battle, the USS *Yorktown* was attacked by Japanese planes.

On June 4, 1942, my father, along with several hundred other survivors, was forced to abandon ship, spending about four hours in the oil-laden water, waiting to be picked up by US destroyers. On my father's flight cap that he wore that day, which we have, you can still smell the oil and seawater soaked into the fabric.

Two days later, a Japanese submarine sent a torpedo into its hull, and the next day the USS *Yorktown* sank. Historians agree that this one infamous battle changed the course of the war in the Pacific.

My father suffered from what we know today as PTSD, which used to be called "shell shock." A personal hell for veterans, regardless of the name. The battles my father fought would echo throughout his life, ultimately influencing some of my own internal wars decades later.

THE BATTLES AFTER THE WAR

My earliest remembrances of my dad are of me sitting in the seat beside him while he was flying his small Cherokee 180 airplane. His greatest passion was flying, the only time he felt truly free.

Almost every day, we were at the airport with his buddies. They spoke the language of flying and shared a common interest in all things aviation. Theirs was an exclusive club—but as my father's son, I felt like a full-fledged member. I knew all his friends by their nicknames and what kinds of airplanes they flew. I can remember stunt pilots and seasoned airline pilots asking my dad about his experiences in the war. Even at a young age, I could sense their respect for him. But like many of his contemporaries, he rarely went into detail about his time in battle.

Hanging around the airport, I always knew that at some point my father would come find me when he was ready to get in the air. By the time I was five, I could read aeronautical charts. My dad taught me how to check the fuel tanks for water and open the cowling to inspect for leaks around the engine. I learned how to gently pull back on the yoke at 80 mph to lift that Cherokee off the runway and how to hold the wings level with the horizon, even before I could see over the dash.

We loved everything about flying, and forty-plus years after his death, I still look to the sky every time I hear a small plane overhead. I squint and shield my eyes from the sun, searching until I find it. I still feel obligated to connect in that small way with my father's sole passion.

My oldest brother was serving on the USS *Oriskany* when the vessel caught fire on the morning of October 26, 1966. The date is etched in my mind because I still remember my parents' anguish as they waited to hear if their son was alive or dead. That event did something in them. The fire aboard the aircraft carrier killed 44 and injured 156 sailors. But my brother was safe. The trauma of watching my parents wait for the news is one of my earliest memories.

When I was around nine years old, my father started having pain in his legs, sometimes to the point of passing out and having to be taken to the hospital by ambulance. All the way into my teenage years, he had multiple surgeries to replace or repair his arteries, which were hardening due to arteriosclerosis. The doctors couldn't stop the spread of the disease that prevented blood flow and caused excruciating pain. He lost his ability to work and later to fly.

I recall waiting in the hospital hallway while my mother and father were consulting with a doctor in another room. When they walked out, my father collapsed against the wall. He had just been told they would have to amputate one leg below the knee. Eventually, they had to amputate the other one below the knee as well to try to stop the relentless spread of gangrene.

Then the "phantom pains" began. Long after the limb was gone, he would scream that his foot was cramping or on fire. He would writhe in pain for days at a time. That whole period is one long, tortuous memory I'll never forget.

Several times toward the end, he begged me to get his pistol for him. I would just run out of the house. I hated watching him hurt the way he did, but I couldn't help him end the pain, especially that way. It took me a long time to shake the guilt of not spending more time with him when he probably needed me the most.

As a teenager, I learned to escape any way I could. I would sneak out my second-floor bedroom window, jump down from the roof, and stay out all night. With all the focus on my dad, my parents never even knew I was gone.

I started drinking, smoking pot, and going way too fast in the car my father couldn't drive anymore. When I was fourteen years old, he tossed me the keys and just said, "Be careful." Fourteen-year-old boys are *not* careful. I honestly don't know how I survived, aside from the diligent work of some guardian angels.

Our pastor would say that God was all-powerful and that He loved me. So of course I started asking Him to make my dad better and fix my family. I reasoned that since God was so great, He could figure something out. But I began to question whether He would respond to an underage drinker who smoked pot and came to church hungover. Maybe no healing came because I couldn't seem to live "the Christian life" very well?

At nine years old, I had walked down the aisle and prayed "the sinner's prayer." Inside the cover of the little Bible that the church gave me was written, "November 9th, 1972." But I would make that trip down to the altar to grovel before God many more times after that.

When I was sixteen years old, on March 11, 1980, my father died.

DRINKING AND DROWNING

My mother had a hard time sleeping after my father's death, having been his caregiver for ten years. She went to see a doctor about her insomnia, and he "prescribed" a glass of wine each night before bed.

Neither of my parents had ever been drinkers. But Mom embraced the doctor's advice like a drowning woman grabs a life vest. Except she did eventually drown, sinking deeper, one day at a time. My mom didn't just drink to get drunk; she drank until she passed out—in the middle of the living room, the front yard, her car in the grocery-store parking lot, or her bed.

I would stay away for days at a time, spending the night with friends. Eventually, my mom was as gone as my father, so I finally moved out to the other side of town and left her to take care of herself.

On the night of December 30, 1990, I stopped by to check on her. All the lights were off in the house. I walked in and called out, only to hear a faint, "Come help me up." Turning on the light, I saw her lying at the bottom of the stairs in a huge pool of blood. At first, I thought she had been shot.

Her head was split open an inch wide all the way down through to the skull from her forehead to the occipital bone on the back of her head. Her eyes were wide open, and of course she reeked of alcohol. The way her head was cocked to the side, I knew something was very wrong. I took her hand but could tell she didn't feel a thing and wasn't moving.

Mom had been lying there for over six hours, which explained why the pool of blood was almost dry. When she had fallen trying to go upstairs, she had hit her head on the doorframe. Her neck was broken.

Ironically, my mother's accident salvaged our relationship and probably kept me from being destroyed by guilt and shame. Being paralyzed from the neck down, she couldn't drink anymore. For a long time, she denied that she was an alcoholic. But one day, out of the blue, Mom said to me, "I'm sorry about my drinking, Tim."

My mother died on October 5, 1996.

THE HEART OF THE FATHER

The day before my mother's accident, I was hanging out at a club. I looked over and saw a girl who was way too beautiful to approach. But after slamming down a few bottles of "liquid courage," I walked over to meet her. Her name was Georgia.

Georgia was stunningly beautiful, which in my insecurity made me feel better about myself, walking around with a girl like her. One of the best things to ever happen to me was when she and I married on July 29, 1994.

She had two boys from her first marriage, so I became an instant dad. Her sons were amazing the day I met them, and they still are. I have always *loved* being their stepdad.

At first, I didn't tell Georgia about me growing up in church. But by our third date, I knew I needed to tell her I was a Christian. When I did, her eyes lit up and she told me about her recent salvation. Our spiritual connection eventually became the foundation of our life together.

At the time, I had no idea how much baggage I was bringing into our relationship. There really is no way you can understand that dynamic until you are living with someone of the opposite sex whom you love and want to please.

FOR BETTER OR FOR WORSE

I mistakenly thought Georgia was just supposed to make me happy, not change me. Being radically different people, especially in those early days, we just confounded each other. And those differences, coupled with unrealistic expectations, created a growing frustration. We didn't know how to communicate in the best of times, and we were even worse at arguing.

Eventually, we had two boys of our own. Now there were four young men looking to me for their example. Needless to say, our lives were incredibly hectic all the time, and we were also neck-deep in church activity. I was on every ministry committee and board while also teaching a large discipleship class.

Slowly, I slipped into the church leader's trap, including a belief in the age-old lie that you can't lead in Churchworld unless you look the part. The main piece of my wardrobe was my mask of perceived perfection. As a couple, Georgia and I were pretending that life was good, though a fuse had been lit from all the problems simmering under the surface in our relationship.

While our marriage was a mess, I got more involved in ministry. I became vice-chairman of the deacons and worked with adults, while Georgia served in the student ministry. As time passed, we began to not even share the same friends.

Eventually, I was asked to join the church staff full-time. At this point, the greatest significance I felt and affirmation I received came from who I was in Churchworld. People saw me as a leader and a good teacher, and this fed me what I craved. My flesh ate it up. But I would never acknowledge the ugliness of my ego.

So I just chalked up the good feelings as a reward from God for being so "selfless." Looking back now, I can clearly see that my motive for virtually everything I did was actually the affirmation. As tough as this is to say now, the glory was mine, not God's.

There's good-looking flesh and then there's ugly flesh. But to God, *both* are flesh, both are ugly, and both are evil at heart. One is acceptable to man's "religion." Neither is acceptable to God. He wants to produce the fruit of His Spirit in us. He wants to reach all the way past our actions, words, and attitudes right down to our motives and change us from the inside out. God wants to become the reason we do ministry that points to Jesus, and the glory is His.

LEADER TO LEPER

My mask, my pretending, and my "acceptable flesh" eventually caught up with me. I had sown plenty—now came the reaping. My entire world came crashing down when Georgia discovered I was having an affair.

Georgia and I entered into the most painful season of our lives. We separated for six months, and I felt like we might not make it. I went to live with my good friend Mike, and Georgia and I started counseling.

In the aftermath of the train wreck, my disguise was stripped away. So I decided to just leave it off. No point in trying to fake my identity any longer. Overnight, I went from a highly respected church leader to a leper. I was shunned and shamed just like those guys who cried out to Jesus for mercy when no one else would come near them.

One day, I threw my Bible down as hard as I could and screamed at God, "You've never been enough for me!"

Experiencing a rare moment of clarity, for the first time in my life, I verbally expressed the disillusionment I had always felt. *Of course, my heavenly Father had known all along.* In that outburst, I confessed that I didn't know how to find life in Christ. And when you can't find life in Him, well, you've got to go get it somewhere else. And I had tried everything.

In the months that followed, the gospel wrapped around me like a warm blanket. During my time alone with God and in His Word, He showed me that I belonged to Him—even on my worst days. He allowed me to see that my standing in Christ had never been based on my own performance. The cross became personal to me for the first time.

God allowed me to see that my standing in Christ had never been based on my own performance.

An incredible weight was lifted off my shoulders, and I finally accepted that God loved me. I didn't need anything *but* Him. All His expectations had already been met in His Son.

TO LOVE AND TO CHERISH

As Georgia and I continued counseling, God did some incredible things in us, and I eventually moved back home. She too had come through much pain in her own journey of transformation. God made us new, teaching Georgia and me how to extend grace to each other and to look only to Him. Jesus began showing us how to find life in Him and then how to give ourselves to each other through His love.

While beginning again was very hard, we started to see a new future for our family. Our four sons had front-row seats to watch God write a new story. And in the end, all six of us were changed. God had purged every drop of the people-pleasing, affirmation-seeking junk out of me. Finally, I was free.

God allowed me to experience total exposure as a fraud so I would be forced to let go of my need for approval from others. He completely transformed the way I understood and received the gospel. Over time, Georgia and I were able to communicate to our boys how God had radically changed both of us.

Today, well over a decade later, we meet with couples often and see that many of them are living from the same futile place we had been. We want to spend the rest of our lives helping people understand the difference between pursuing dead religion and being transformed by Jesus.

The Lord can change whatever your situation may be. What He has done for me, He can do for you. I want to help men know how God can turn the hearts of fathers to their children and the hearts of children to their fathers, just like He promised.

The old saying "Life either makes you better or bitter" is so true. We take what has been handed to us and make our own choices. We repent or repeat. Yet the Bible is filled with "But God" verses and divine turning points. Mine finally arrived when I realized my heavenly Father had always been pursuing me with His love and grace.

Part One

FATHER

Chapter 3

The Father's Covenant

I (Tim) grew up in a mainline denominational church in the Bible Belt. Our pastor was a good man who loved God and preached straight out of Scripture every Sunday. At the end of his sermon, he would always walk down front while the music minister led everyone in singing the first and last stanzas of one of the old hymns like "Just as I Am."

By the time I was a teenager struggling with identity and losing the battle against all kinds of temptations, the guilt and shame from what I had done on Friday and Saturday nights would catch up to me in that pew on Sunday mornings. I had a youth pastor who greatly inspired me, and I wanted to be just like him. I so wanted to be the kind of guy who honored God, but I constantly struggled. There was *always* a spiritual tension in my soul.

All the other guys in my youth group appeared to understand things in a way that I just couldn't seem to grasp. My motivation to try to change was an underlying fear. But that can work only for a little while, and it never affected my real desires. Every year, we would go on summer youth retreats. And every single time, I would get so convicted and so fired up that I would make a grand declaration about the person I was going to be when I returned home. But the change never stuck.

To be honest, the Christian life seemed more of a burden to me than a blessing. I felt like I was always chasing a carrot that stayed just out of my reach. Internally, I resigned myself to the belief that the reason I couldn't seem to find the Jesus I heard others talk about was that I wasn't performing well enough for Him.

I lost count of all the times I walked the aisle at the invitation to talk to the pastor while the choir sang. Several times I prayed the sinner's prayer "just to be sure." Sometimes I decided to rededicate my life … again. Looking back, I wonder how many church members said to one another, "There goes Tim. Is he *ever* going to get it?"

I remember hearing sermons in church like the infamous "sin in the camp" story from Joshua 7. The bottom line was that, because a guy named Achan disobeyed God by hiding some forbidden things in his tent, God had the Israelites kill him and his whole family. The scary part was that I knew I had forbidden things in my tent too. I had secret sins hidden in my life that no one knew about.

So applying this Old Testament story to me, I could never seem to shake the idea that God was mad and probably out to get me, just like Achan. Those thoughts seriously haunted me at night as I lay in bed.

I could never seem to shake the idea that God was mad and probably out to get me.

But sometimes my pastor would teach out of the New Testament about how Jesus loved me and died for my sins. This back-and-forth spiritual tug-of-war made me feel like God was angry one minute, then warm and fuzzy the next. I became convinced that salvation was always tied to behavior. Only good works could appease the angry God, while bad behavior caused that same God to distance Himself. The Old Testament always seemed to eclipse the New Testament to me. And my sinful behavior always overshadowed everything I wanted to believe about the gospel.

So in my heart I was always asking, *Are there two different Gods? Which one am I dealing with?*

The elephant in the room was that my worldview put the burden of my salvation partly on me. God was God, so He could do His part, but I felt like I had to work to get the rest of the way to Him. While I don't remember consciously thinking in those terms, I carried that internal burden. In my mind was this future version of me who would someday make the cut with God. But I never knew how to become that guy.

Those questions made me constantly insecure about my standing before God, because I knew I wasn't measuring up. Saturday-night drinking caused Sunday-morning hangovers. Fear and guilt were the tools others always seemed to use to motivate me to be a better person. What was so strange and so frustrating was that the guilt I felt was never able to give me the fuel to be the kind of Christian I heard at church I was supposed to be!

So I lived in a vicious cycle of shame, wanting God's love and approval but never feeling like I could meet His standard. If I could only "try harder" to be a Christian, then one day everything would be made right. I always told myself that I needed a little more time to get some area of my life together, and then I would meet God's expectation.

Needless to say, I stumbled into my adult life confused about the gospel and my salvation. This profoundly impacted my relationship with God, my ability to love people, and even the way I sometimes shared my twisted and broken version of the gospel with others. Ironically, I could clearly articulate what the Bible teaches about sin and salvation, but intimacy with God was a total mystery to me.

Two things I know in hindsight: First, all of this massively impacted my ability to receive my wife's love, and that alone created all sorts of problems for us. And second, through all those years, I never understood the old covenant versus the new covenant and how Jesus had built the bridge between the two.

COVENANT VS. CONSUMER

I meet people all the time who have the same concept of God that I had. There are evidently a lot of us "Achans" out there waiting for the sin in our tents to be discovered and judgment to fall. And as fathers, we must get this right so we can pass truth on to our kids.

As a father, you will hand over to your children the gospel that you understand. You will paint for your children the same picture of God that you have in your head. This isn't psychological mumbo jumbo. This is reality. That is why we need to allow the Holy Spirit to teach us through God's Word and accept who we became when He adopted us into His family. We've got to learn to recognize and acknowledge how and why our concept of God may be broken and allow Him to show us who He truly is.

As a father, you will hand over to your children the gospel that you understand. You will paint for your children the same picture of God that you have in your head.

Through incredible brokenness in my life, God convinced me that the gospel was actually good news. Trust me: it is *really* good news. He has an amazing answer to this overwhelming problem of ours.

The only time we seem to hear the word "covenant" these days is during some wedding ceremonies. But to truly understand the nature of our relationship with God, we have to first grasp the meaning of a biblical covenant. Why? Because it's the *only* kind of relationship God has with us. Anything else is just religion—man trying to find God on his own terms.

Pastor and apologist Timothy Keller teaches that a covenant relationship is one where both parties commit to each other:

- "I'm going to be what I should be."
- "I'm going to do what I should do."
- "I will uphold my end of the agreement whether you uphold yours or not."

The first time I heard Keller teach God's covenant relationship in a sermon, this truth was a game changer for me. In all my years in church, I had never heard covenant connected to what Christ accomplished on the cross.

The key is that both parties must have the same attitude and resolve toward each other. If not, you can end up with an imbalanced, even abusive, relationship. When both agree to a covenant relationship, we see a beautiful picture of the gospel. However, for this relationship to be sustainable, there have to be consequences, penalties for not keeping the covenant.

Years ago, I was a real estate broker. I constantly handled people's earnest money that they would put down when they signed a contract. The legal language was clear that if they backed out of that contract then they would lose their earnest money. Not keeping their end of the deal was going to cost them.

Earnest money provides the accountability *and* the penalty. Contracts would be weak and difficult to enforce if there were no consequences for *not* doing what you promised to do. To summarize, in a covenant relationship:

- There is a promise and there is a penalty.
- You have a promise to keep.
- You have a penalty to pay if you break your promise.

The majority of our relationships today are consumer relationships, not covenant relationships. If your mechanic doesn't fix your car and won't make things right, you find another mechanic. If a new grocery store is built in your community with better prices and shorter checkout lines than the one you've been going to, you just switch stores. If you don't like how the barber cuts your hair, you go to another one next time.

In a consumer relationship, you are all about what is best for you. *You* are first. And because most of our relationships are consumer relationships, the nature of a covenant relationship is countercultural to almost everything we experience today.

A covenant relationship is all about what is best for the *relationship* with the other person, not what you can get out of the other person. You are second. As human beings, we manipulate others all the time to try to get what we want or need. But that is sin's way, not God's.

In Genesis 15, we find God's covenant with a man named Abram, later known as Abraham, the father of the Jewish nation. Here we read about a fascinating and beautiful foreshadowing of the gospel.

God told Abram He was going to enter into a covenant relationship with him. Because of the cultural traditions in that day, Abram knew that if two people wanted to enter into a covenant relationship, they would participate in a specific sacrifice known as the "cutting ceremony."

God instructed Abram to gather some animals, kill and cut them in half, and then lay the severed halves out on the ground in two rows, creating an aisle to walk down through the middle between the parts. *Yes, this would have been a bloody, grisly scene.*

During this ceremony, one man would start at the top and walk down through the pieces of the sacrifice to the halfway point.

The other man would walk from the other direction and the two would meet in the middle, signifying their equal commitment. This was intended to communicate that if one or the other did not keep his promise, he would be cut to pieces just like the animals.

But for Abram, after cutting and laying out the animals as instructed, something extraordinary happened while he waited on God.

> It came about, when the sun had set, that it was very dark, and behold, a smoking oven and a flaming torch appeared which passed between these pieces. On that day the LORD made a covenant with Abram, saying,

> "To your descendants I have given this land,
>   From the river of Egypt as far as the great river,
>   the river Euphrates." (Gen. 15:17–18 NASB)

God put Abram into a deep sleep, and darkness fell around him, signifying judgment. God then moved down through the sacrifice—all the way from top to bottom, between the halves—while Abram did nothing.

Yes, Abram did *nothing*. In this covenant ceremony, God signified to Abram and his descendants that if God Himself didn't keep His promise, God would be sacrificed or torn to pieces like those animals. What an incredibly powerful picture and promise!

But here is the most amazing aspect of this story: by walking all the way through the sacrifice, God also signified that if Abram or his descendants didn't keep their promise, God alone would be torn to pieces—sacrificed. God put all the burden of the covenant on Himself! He communicated that in this covenant relationship, if we broke the covenant, He would pay the penalty for our inability, and even our unwillingness, to keep the covenant. Don't miss that! God Himself promised to pay the penalty!

This scene is one of the first connections we have of the problem of sin presented in the Old Testament to the Answer given in the New Testament. The apostle Paul addressed this paradigm often in his teaching.

> Well then, should we conclude that we Jews are bet-
> ter than others? No, not at all, for we have already
> shown that all people, whether Jews or Gentiles, are
> under the power of sin. As the Scriptures say,
>
> "No one is righteous—
>   not even one.
> No one is truly wise;
>   no one is seeking God." ...
>
> Obviously, the law applies to those to whom
> it was given, for its purpose is to keep people
> from having excuses, and to show that the entire
> world is guilty before God. For no one can ever
> be made right with God by doing what the law
> commands. The law simply shows us how sinful
> we are. (Rom. 3:9–11, 19–20)

Connecting the covenant ceremony back to my own struggle, I kept thinking that God was standing at the halfway point of the covenant, angry that I couldn't manage to walk out my part. I didn't yet understand that He had already fulfilled the entire covenant out of His grace and love.

THE CREATION OF THE NEW COVENANT

When the Roman Empire ruled the Western world, one of their favorite methods of execution was crucifixion. The first step in carrying out a crucifixion was to beat the prisoner with a cat-o'-nine-tails, a whip with chunks of broken glass, sharp rocks, and pieces of bone tied to the ends of its leather strips.

As His time on earth drew to a close, Jesus was sentenced to be crucified. We know that Roman soldiers "flogged" or "scourged" Jesus, possibly with the cat-o'-nine-tails (John 19:1).

When those shards of bone, rock, and glass struck Jesus' body, they would've torn into His flesh. When the torturer drew the whip back, Jesus' skin would've been ripped open from side to side across His entire back. While the Bible does not say how many lashes Jesus was given, Jewish law stated that forty would kill most men. So to ensure that a man would not die until he was on the cross, they would stop at thirty-nine.

Following such a brutal and horrific beating and whipping, Jesus would have been "cut and torn to pieces," much like the sacrificial animals had been in the cutting ceremony.

Next came the task of carrying the crossbeam to Golgotha, the place where the execution would be carried out. In the final phase of the crucifixion, spikes were driven through the wrists and ankles to be certain His bones would secure Him as He hung on the cross. The Son of God was sacrificed—walking all the way through the pieces—for our sin.

Remember the darkness that fell when Abram slept to signify God's judgment? "At noon, darkness fell across the whole land until three o'clock" (Matt. 27:45). God placed all our judgment, all His anger over sin, onto His Son.

> Surely he took up our pain
>   and bore our suffering,
> yet we considered him punished by God,
>   stricken by him, and afflicted.
> But he was pierced for our transgressions,
>   he was crushed for our iniquities;
> the punishment that brought us peace was on him,
>   and by his wounds we are healed.
> We all, like sheep, have gone astray,
>   each of us has turned to our own way;
> and the LORD has laid on him
>   the iniquity of us all. (Isa. 53:4–6 NIV)

In the Old Testament, we read that God had given the law as the penalty for sin. In the New Testament we read that Jesus took the penalty to satisfy the law once and for all so we wouldn't have to die spiritually.

> First, Christ said, "You did not want animal sac-
> rifices or sin offerings or burnt offerings or other

offerings for sin, nor were you pleased with them"
(though they are required by the law of Moses).
Then he said, "Look, I have come to do your will."
He cancels the first covenant in order to put the
second into effect. For God's will was for us to
be made holy by the sacrifice of the body of Jesus
Christ, once for all time. (Heb. 10:8–10)

GOD'S PROMISE, NOT YOUR PERFORMANCE

If you are a Christian, you are in a covenant relationship with
God. The good news is that this relationship is not held together
by your ability to keep your promises, because it's not about your
performance.

God kept His promise (i.e., fulfilled this covenant) by paying
the penalty for us, providing His blessing to us. We can be confident
that our standing before God will never change or be affected by our
failures.

Please allow this truth to sink in on a deep, personal level. Jesus
lived the perfect life that God requires of you and me. He died for
our sins, but He also lived for our righteousness. Your standing
before God is based on His perfect performance! That's *really* good
news. There should be no fear in our hearts when we think of how
God views us, even on our worst day in our worst moment. "For
God has not given us a spirit of fear and timidity, but of power, love,
and self-discipline" (2 Tim. 1:7).

Some folks say that if you talk too much about God's grace,
people will use that as an excuse to sin. In our men's ministry, we

jokingly call this the "hookers and heroin phenomenon." The reason-
ing is that if the grace of God is emphasized too much, men will go
out and solicit hookers and do heroin. The fear is that they will get the
idea that since they are saved, they can live as they please. Of course,
that's not at all what happens when the gospel captures a man's heart.

Paul anticipated that very response when he wrote about the
matchless grace of God in Romans 5 and 6. The first verses of chapter 6 are a great example: "Well then, should we keep on sinning so
that God can show us more and more of his wonderful grace? Of
course not!"

Sin is never acceptable. But until we realize that we are free from
condemnation, we will never truly draw close to God, because we
think He is still angry with us.

Due to my own lack of understanding, I never communicated
this revelation to my kids when they were younger. The gospel they
got from me was quite different from the true gospel. So I had to have
some intentional conversations with them. I couldn't just change
overnight and pretend like I had always understood the covenant.

Sitting them down and talking them through what God had
taught me, I had to give them some painful examples of times I
knew I hadn't communicated a covenant love for them. I wanted
them to clearly see and understand the difference between what I had
understood before and what I had come to understand.

Dad, hitting the restart button may take some humility on your
part to communicate to your kids that you have missed this truth in
the past. But this could also cause a monumental shift in the life of
your family and in their hearts and minds.

M46 Dads Challenge Three

Dad, ask your children these two questions:

> 1. Do you believe there is anything you could do that would make me love you less?
> 2. Do you believe there is anything you could do that would make me love you more?

In your own words and in your own way, explain to your children that God's love for those who are in Christ is based on what Jesus has accomplished through His sacrifice and performance, not on their own ability to perform.

Tell them that your love for them is the same.

Say the words to them.

Fight for the hearts of your children!

Todd and Zack's M46 Moment

Fighting for Love, Not Perfection

TODD

During my son Zack's sophomore year in high school, I started attending the M46 meetings led by Kenny Dallas and Tim Sexton. I especially connected to Coach Dallas because I had also coached football. At every CRASH session, we received a challenge we were to do with our kids.

At one particular CRASH, they told us to sit down at the dinner table and ask our sons and daughters this question: "Do you think there is anything you could do that would make me love you more or less?" They instructed us to just sit and listen, keep our mouths shut, let the kids speak, take it in, and if necessary, ask for forgiveness.

I accepted the challenge. At dinner, I asked Zack the question—and he *blasted* me. Or at least that's the way it felt in the moment.

"Dad," Zack said, "you wore me out *at home* about football, on the way *to* football, and then *at* football practice! Then you wore me out all the way home *from* football! You never stopped! It never ended. Nothing I did was ever good enough! You made me play against guys two years older than me. You always made me hit the hardest players on the team."

Then my boy delivered the knockout punch: "Dad, I ... hated ... football! Absolutely hated ... football!"

The entire time, I was trying to hold back the tears. Of course, as a dad who deeply loves his son, I never meant to do *anything* to hurt him. But on that day, I realized I had been hurting him his entire life.

I'd been coaching Zack since he was three years old, and he was then sixteen. That's a lot of years to hate something you're doing. Having to do something for all the wrong reasons.

Finally, I couldn't hold back the tears any longer. "Zack, please forgive me! I am so sorry!"

My son responded, "I already forgave you. But also, Dad, if it wasn't for you and what you did, I wouldn't be the man I am today."

In that very tough moment of truth, my relationship with my son was restored. But here's the kicker: I didn't know our relationship was broken until I asked the question from the M46 Dads Challenge. How long would Zack have gone without telling me the truth? Would he *ever* have told me? How long would I have gone on not knowing?

But I did ask, and he answered with honesty. While the truth hurts, it can also set us free.

The M46 CRASH Courses changed my life, as well as the relationship between me and my son, by challenging me to ask him just one simple question—the right question.

I knew immediately I had to change my behavior so that football was about Zack and not me. I stopped going to his practices. And after games, I just told him how awesome he played. Sometimes he would say, "Don't lie, Dad. You know I stunk it up out there." And we would just laugh. Because we had been set free to focus on our relationship.

My son went far past my expectations in football. He was a three-year starter, winning three state championships in a row. He had a couple of offers to play football in college but declined.

I firmly believe that if I had not asked my challenge question, he likely would have continued on and played football … just to please me. That is exactly what I had expected of him and had wanted him to do. But man, was I ever wrong! That M46 Moment allowed me to see and understand the pressure I had put on my son for way too many years and how that had made him feel.

Today, Zack and I have intimate conversations where we can feel the love that we have for each other. He is now able to talk to me and express anything. Praise God!

M46 encouraged me to listen and obey what God wants. I'm not ashamed to say that Christ changed my life. I am grateful to M46 Dads for a restored relationship with my son, and I owe everything to Jesus for making it *all* possible.

ZACK

When I was growing up, my dad made sure of two things: One was that I served God. He made sure I served God by always setting a godly example, taking our family to church, and spending time in the Word to discern how to lead us in the best possible way.

And two, he made sure I played football. He was always my coach. Some people might think having your dad as the coach would be easy. But from the son's perspective, this can be one of the most challenging things to grow up with. I was always treated differently than the rest of my teammates, and the expectations on me were higher than on anyone else.

My dad and I always had the best relationship—except when it came time to call him "Coach." How can any athlete perform at his maximum ability with the insane amount of pressure of wanting to always satisfy his dad?

But everything changed my sophomore year of high school. M46 Dads launched, and my father went every time the doors were open. As he continued to go to the meetings, he also opened up opportunities for us to really talk and be honest. After one specific conversation, for the first time, I was able to play the game I loved with zero anxiety or stress over how well I played.

My dad began to see the game from a different perspective and was able to cheer me on without any instruction or finding fault. Where he used to fight for *perfection*, he began fighting for *love*. He let me know that as long as I loved what I was doing, he was content. He understood that my desires are not always his desires. That change made the pressure fall off my shoulders like links from a chain. He developed a love for just being a fan, and that allowed me to excel.

Through this, our relationship only grew closer. I was able to come to my dad in situations where before I would never have been able to confide in him. M46 Dads changed not only my dad's life but mine too.

M46 Dads changed not only my dad's life but mine too.

Chapter 4

Religious Pursuit vs. Gospel Transformation

After being a believer for many years, I (Tim) came to the painful realization that my concept of what the Christian life is really all about was not working. A personal crisis put me at a spiritual crossroads, forcing me to ask, "What exactly do I believe, and what difference does my faith make?"

I finally arrived at the conclusion that I had spent my life as a believer *pursuing religion* rather than engaging in a *transforming relationship* with Jesus Christ. I was busy doing, not being. I was involved in religious activity that was not changing me internally. I offered up an image of myself that I wanted people to see, but it didn't match the person I knew I actually was.

When we read the Gospels, we find that Jesus repeatedly addressed the religious leaders of His day for doing the same thing.

> You blind Pharisee! First clean the inside of the cup and the plate, that the outside also may be clean.
>
> Woe to you, scribes and Pharisees, hypocrites! For you are like whitewashed tombs, which outwardly

appear beautiful, but within are full of dead people's bones and all uncleanness. So you also outwardly appear righteous to others, but within you are full of hypocrisy and lawlessness. (Matt. 23:26–28 ESV)

When I use the word "religion," I'm talking about the attempt to perform our way into a right standing with God. But this effort is pointless and impossible.

For years, I'd been very familiar with this verse from Paul: "For everyone has sinned; we all fall short of God's glorious standard" (Rom. 3:23). But it wasn't until I had my own crisis that the verses just before and after verse 23 began to sink in:

We are made right with God by placing our faith in Jesus Christ. And this is true for everyone who believes, no matter who we are.…

Yet God, in his grace, freely makes us right in his sight. He did this through Christ Jesus when he freed us from the penalty for our sins. (Rom. 3:22, 24)

Phrases like "made right," "no matter who we are," and "freed us from the penalty" took root in my heart. These truths talked about God's work for me, not my work for Him.

My heavenly Father was gracious to hear all my questions and lead me to His answers. He met me right where I was, with all my struggles and doubts. The encounter of seeking Him at a deeper level changed my life. The journey caused me to truly see and understand the simplicity and authenticity of the gospel for the first time.

This, of course, also impacted the way I communicated the truth of Christ to my children. From my own experience, I can say that every lie we believe, every truth of His that we grasp, every act of hypocrisy we do, and every opportunity we take to draw near to God's heart will also be seen, heard, and experienced by our kids. That alone should be a major spiritual motivator for us as dads.

Every lie we believe, every truth of God's that we grasp, every act of hypocrisy we do, and every opportunity we take to draw near to God's heart will also be seen, heard, and experienced by our kids.

Before we move on, please allow me to repeat this statement for emphasis: there is a massive difference between *pursuing religion* and being *transformed* by the *gospel*.

INTIMACY VS. INSECURITY

Over the years of ministering to men from all walks of life, I have discovered there are a lot of us struggling with religion the same way I did. Not knowing any better. Not understanding the difference.

And also, just like me, many of us are becoming more frustrated and disillusioned by the day. Rather than finding answers, the questions just keep mounting. Trust me, I get it.

As men of faith, regardless of our spiritual maturity, what we all truly want is for our kids to know and love God. We want them to be transformed by the gospel. None of us want to see our children carry the burden of dead religion. We hope to see them experience intimacy with their heavenly Father.

Yet as dads, we cannot give something away that we ourselves do not have. If we don't recognize truth, we will transfer that same performance-based, fear-motivated religion to our children, like a bad strand of family DNA. And the vicious cycle will continue with the next generation.

How many people do you know who say they are Christians and yet their faith just doesn't seem to be making a big difference in their lives? The question is not about passing judgment but rather about being honest about evidence. As always, Jesus said it best: "Yes, just as you can identify a tree by its fruit, so you can identify people by their actions" (Matt. 7:20).

Let's say you have two apple trees—one with plastic fruit that someone has placed on the branches and the other with actual apples produced on its own. If someone bumps into both trees, which one's fruit falls off? The apples that are just decorations will fall to the ground because they are not actually part of the tree. Real fruit comes from the tree itself and doesn't fall off when the tree is shaken.

God doesn't want us faking fruit. He wants to produce in us fruit that grows out of our intimate relationship with Him. He doesn't want us showing people who we wish we were, pretending we're patient, forgiving, or compassionate. God wants to mold us more and more into the image of His Son. He wants to authentically produce those attributes, the good fruit, *in* and *through* us. This happens as we understand His ways and trust Him through obedience. Living for Christ is not about willpower or sheer discipline but a changed heart.

Have you ever been in a relationship with someone and you never seemed to know exactly where you stood? A parent, coach, boss, coworker, friend, or girlfriend? You find yourself constantly afraid that if you offend that person or mess up in any way, he or she will write you off or reject you entirely. You feel like you're always walking on eggshells.

That type of relationship is built on insecurity. In such a situation, will you ever experience true closeness with that person? No, of course not. The reason? Insecurity is the enemy of intimacy.

There are people both inside and outside the church who have that same insecurity in their relationships with God. I know I certainly did. So where does this originate? What does the Bible say about the remedy for this condition?

Because God cannot tolerate sin and we are all born into sin, we are alive physically and mentally, but dead spiritually. We are separated from God by our nature or state of sin that began with Adam.

After God had created Adam and placed him in the garden, He gave this one rule: "But the LORD God warned him, 'You may freely eat the fruit of every tree in the garden—except the tree of the knowledge of good and evil. If you eat its fruit, you are sure to die'" (Gen. 2:16–17).

God gave Adam dominion over all of creation. "Then the LORD God said, 'It is not good for the man to be alone. I will make a helper who is just right for him'" (Gen. 2:18). God made woman to join the man. Together, the two original humans had a direct connection to Him with no obstacles or barriers of any kind. They were naked and unashamed, not at all self-aware.

But as we know, in Genesis 3, God's mutinous enemy tempted Eve. Adam chose to follow rather than lead, and the rest is history. God's one command was disobeyed, and consequences were born.

God had warned that if they ate the fruit they were "sure to die." But Adam and Eve didn't die that day. In fact, they lived many, many more years. So did anything die when they disobeyed God? Yes: their fellowship with God. They were separated from Him because of sin. The direct fellowship and connection were severed because of their choice.

You and I were born into the family lineage of Adam. We are his descendants. We exit the womb with an inherited sin nature, separated from God. But the bad news just gets worse, because to gain access to God, we must be made right with Him by achieving absolute perfection in actions and thoughts.

Let's get a little more backstory now on how sin was forgiven before Jesus arrived. And, Dad, remember: all of what we are talking about in this chapter, as theologically thick as it may seem, is critical to how we see God and also how we present Him to our children.

FROM A TENT TO A TEMPLE

In 2 Samuel 6, we read the account of King David who, along with thirty thousand troops, attempted to move the Ark of the Covenant on an oxen cart back to their home in Jerusalem. As they sang loudly and celebrated through praise and worship, suddenly the oxen stumbled. Reacting without thinking, a man named Uzzah reached out to grab the Ark to steady it. As soon as he touched the Ark, he fell dead. That's a quick way to end a worship service, huh? Why did Uzzah suddenly die?

Long before this event, God had given specific instructions to Moses and Aaron not to allow anyone to touch what was holy, in this case the Ark of the Covenant. The real issue was not Uzzah's action but God's perfection that cannot tolerate disobedience—intentional or not.

Habakkuk 1:13 states, "But you are pure and cannot stand the sight of evil." Throughout the Old Testament, we are shown time and time again that God hates sin, while in the New Testament, we are constantly pointed toward Jesus' sacrifice as payment for our sin.

In 1 Chronicles 17, there is a transcription of a conversation between God and Nathan the prophet regarding a desire of King David's. The king had decided that God's Ark should no longer be in a tent but in a permanent, beautiful house. David wanted to build this house, this temple. But God told Nathan to tell David that God didn't need a home—yet. God added that David's son Solomon would one day build a great temple for Him.

In 1 Kings 5, Solomon took on the construction of the Temple in Jerusalem, based on very specific and detailed instructions from God. Here are the basics of the Temple and how that pertains to us today:

First, there was the Outer Court, where anyone was free to gather.

Next, there was the Inner Court, where only priests could enter.

Last, there was the Holy of Holies, where only the High Priest could enter, and then only one time per year.

That annual event was called the Day of Atonement, and it was the day when the sacrifice for sin was made before God. The actual ritual included burning incense, lighting lamps, and offering animal sacrifices. These animal deaths were the substitution for the death of the people for their sins. Blood had to be shed. Something had to die in exchange for forgiveness and atonement.

> For without the shedding of blood, there is no forgiveness.
> That is why the Tabernacle [Temple] and everything in it, which were copies of things in heaven, had to be purified by the blood of animals. (Heb. 9:22–23)

The night before the Day of Atonement, the priest went through a cleansing ceremony in which he washed his body five times and his hands and feet ten times. At the appointed time, the High Priest walked into the Holy of Holies carrying a bucket of animal blood as part of the sacrifice.

The Holy of Holies, a closet-sized area at the heart of the Temple, was revered as the one sinless place on earth, the place where God's presence came down. While the High Priest was of course a sinner, his Levite bloodline, priestly training, and years of building credibility in the ranks would allow him to offer the atonement.

But what made the Holy of Holies *holy* was God's manifest presence. This unique occurrence had been seen with Moses as God's presence was in the cloud by day, fire by night, and the Tent of Meeting.

Another important detail is that at the entrance to the Holy of Holies was a curtain, sixty feet wide, thirty feet high, and four inches thick, separating everyone but the High Priest from the presence of God.

FROM A PLACE TO A PERSON

Now, let's fast-forward a few thousand years. Jesus came to earth and lived a perfect life. He had no sin, despite living in the midst of the evils of humanity. He remained 100 percent holy.

When the appointed time came for Christ's sacrifice, He was arrested, executed, and buried. Three days later, He walked out from the tomb, just as was prophesied in the Old Testament and as He had promised His disciples. In His resurrected body, Jesus appeared to at least five hundred witnesses over a forty-day period.

On the night before His death, Christ made an intriguing promise:

> And I will ask the Father, and he will give you another Advocate, who will never leave you. He is the Holy Spirit, who leads into all truth. The world cannot receive him, because it isn't looking for him and doesn't recognize him. But you know him, because he lives with you now and later will be in you. (John 14:16–17)

Pay attention to that last sentence: "He lives with you now and later will be in you." Catch the shift from *with* you to *in* you.

Look at these words from the apostle Paul:

> Don't you realize that all of you together are the
> temple of God and that the Spirit of God lives in
> you? God will destroy anyone who destroys this
> temple. For God's temple is holy, and you are that
> temple. (1 Cor. 3:16–17)

See it? The Holy Spirit comes to live in us, making *us* God's new temple. His dwelling place shifts from being a place to being a person, starting with Jesus. We no longer have to go to the Temple or have a priest represent us before God. We become the temple by the work of Christ.

When your kids come into their own relationships with Jesus, they become the temple where God dwells too. They must know and understand this truth, even though their minds, behavior, and everything around them will scream that it is not true.

> But now Jesus, our High Priest, has been given a min-
> istry that is far superior to the old priesthood, for he
> is the one who mediates for us a far better covenant
> with God, based on better promises. (Heb. 8:6)

> And you are living stones that God is building into
> his spiritual temple. What's more, you are his holy
> priests. Through the mediation of Jesus Christ, you
> offer spiritual sacrifices that please God. (1 Pet. 2:5)

Through the cross and resurrection, Jesus offers His perfect life in exchange for our imperfect lives. The theological term for this trade is known as "imputed righteousness." Christ's perfect performance removes our poor performance the moment we are redeemed. Also, what is called "justification" is the fact that Jesus' sacrifice brought about the justice that God required for our sin, and we can accept His death and life as our own.

We are alive to God, with nothing hindering the connection. While we cannot return to the physical location of Eden, we can now live in the same *spiritual state* as Adam and Eve's original condition.

Dad, realize that this is also your spiritual condition as a child of God in Christ. Do your children recognize that, even as they struggle in this fallen world, they too are the temple of God?

> For God made Christ, who never sinned, to be the
> offering for our sin, so that we could be made right
> with God through Christ. (2 Cor. 5:21)

On the cross, God treated Jesus like He had lived our lives of sin. But now, He treats us as if we live Jesus' life every day. This is the heart and transformational power of the gospel.

But here is the major difference between our state in Christ as redeemed and restored people and Adam and Eve's original state in Eden—we still have our sinful:

- Mind (thinker)
- Will (chooser)
- Emotions (feeler)

So the questions of the ages are: If I am righteous in God's sight now, then why do I still sin? And why do I sin so often? Why do my children, who belong to God, still struggle with sin so much?

The answer is that God doesn't remove our ability to sin. Rather, He gives us His Spirit to now offer a new choice—the same choice Adam and Eve had prior to when the enemy showed up. They were fully connected to God, but He gave them the free will to choose Him or to sin. They were not robots.

In the same way, when we are in Christ, we are fully connected to God. He gives us the moment-by-moment choice between Him and sin. We can choose to walk in the flesh or in the Spirit. We are not robots either.

God gives us the moment-by-moment choice between Him and sin.

Thank God the apostle Paul was so transparent and honest about the deep struggle this constant choice can be.

> I have discovered this principle of life—that when I want to do what is right, I inevitably do what is wrong. I love God's law with all my heart. But there is another power within me that is at war with my mind. This power makes me a slave to the sin that is

still within me. Oh, what a miserable person I am! Who will free me from this life that is dominated by sin and death? Thank God! The answer is in Jesus Christ our Lord. So you see how it is: In my mind I really want to obey God's law, but because of my sinful nature I am a slave to sin. (Rom. 7:21–25)

But look at how Paul resolved the struggle:

So now there is no condemnation for those who belong to Christ Jesus. And because you belong to him, the power of the life-giving Spirit has freed you from the power of sin that leads to death. (Rom. 8:1–2)

Remember the massive curtain that separated the Holy of Holies from the people? Check out what happened when Jesus died on the cross: "Then Jesus shouted out again, and he released his spirit. At that moment the curtain in the sanctuary of the Temple was torn in two, from top to bottom" (Matt. 27:50–51).

In Christ, God's presence erupted from the Holy of Holies in the Temple and spilled into the Outer Court. God's Spirit moved from a place to the people.

BATTLING OUR BAGGAGE

A relationship with Christ does not automatically remove our harmful baggage. Sometimes God will deliver someone from an addiction or personal struggle at the moment of salvation, but such testimonies are rare.

The emotional and spiritual issues, along with past pain, choices, and wrong ideas we have been taught, shown, or have come to believe about God, travel with us as we cross from spiritual death to spiritual life. But as we begin our journey with Jesus, He will start to address them.

While some people were blessed to be raised in loving homes where the gospel was demonstrated, others were abused in some form and have a very skewed concept of God. We each begin our walks with Jesus from different places.

But no matter where we start, we are all going to the same destination. Once we enter into a relationship with Christ, we are in the same process—sanctification. This will look somewhat different in each of us, but God will, over time, make very real changes in our minds, wills, and emotions by the presence of His Spirit. Our transformation into the image of Jesus will continue until we enter heaven's gates, where we are made complete once and for all.

The paradox of Christianity is that we will always deal with sinful behavior, though God now views us as holy. He considers us to be justified and redeemed, even though we still struggle and fail. But the incredibly good news is that God has made us right with Him through the finished work of His Son.

So let's get personal: Have you lived with the lie, like I once did, that if you can just get your act together and clean up your life, you'll be good in God's eyes? Or how about this one: "Once I take care of some of these issues, then I can approach God"?

That makes as much sense as absolutely totaling your car and yet telling yourself you'll have it drivable again soon if you work on it in your garage on weekends. You remove as many dents as possible by yourself before giving up and taking it to the body shop. That is exactly what so many people decide about their baggage: they attempt to "fix it" before giving it to God.

After we come to Christ, we can take all our nastiness and just lay it before Him. He already knows what is there, even better than we do, and knows exactly what to do with it.

Another lie I often hear is that someone thinks he is right with God just because he is morally better than someone else. That is a very dangerous false gospel. The thought that we can somehow become disciplined people who get good at checking all the boxes and being morally superior compared to others is biblically wrong.

Unfortunately, in the church we have placed a premium on the appearance of morality and have not emphasized the posture of the heart. Plenty of men truly love Jesus, but when pressure is applied to their lives, they reach for some form of escape.

One of my friends has cigar burns on his back from when his alcoholic father would "discipline" him. A friend exposed him to drugs when he was around twelve, and he realized that his fear and anxiety went away when he got high. And now as an adult, that is his greatest battle when things get tough. He wants so badly to reach for chemical relief.

I know other men who would never touch alcohol or drugs, but they are in crushing debt because they desperately need to buy "nice things" so people will perceive them as successful.

All of these responses to life are evidence of baggage. God is always working to free His children from those chains of bondage. We are right with God because of Jesus, not because we have everything together. And not because we *look* like we have everything together.

Jesus exposed this lie in His encounter with a Pharisee named Nicodemus. The Pharisees were religious leaders known for being "good" externally. But Jesus referred to them as whitewashed tombs—clean on the outside but dead on the inside. Nicodemus was intrigued by Jesus' teachings, so he approached Christ with his questions.

> "Rabbi," he said, "we all know that God has sent you to teach us. Your miraculous signs are evidence that God is with you."
>
> Jesus replied, "I tell you the truth, unless you are born again, you cannot see the Kingdom of God."
>
> "What do you mean?" exclaimed Nicodemus. "How can an old man go back into his mother's womb and be born again?"
>
> Jesus replied, "I assure you, no one can enter the Kingdom of God without being born of water and the Spirit. Humans can reproduce only human life, but the Holy Spirit gives birth to spiritual life. So don't be surprised when I say, 'You must be born again.' The wind blows wherever it wants. Just as you can hear the wind but can't tell where it comes from or where it is going, so you can't explain how people are born of the Spirit."
>
> "How are these things possible?" Nicodemus asked.
>
> Jesus replied, "You are a respected Jewish teacher, and yet you don't understand these things?

I assure you, we tell you what we know and have seen, and yet you won't believe our testimony. But if you don't believe me when I tell you about earthly things, how can you possibly believe if I tell you about heavenly things? No one has ever gone to heaven and returned. But the Son of Man has come down from heaven. And as Moses lifted up the bronze snake on a pole in the wilderness, so the Son of Man must be lifted up, so that everyone who believes in him will have eternal life." (John 3:2–15)

Nicodemus carried some serious religious baggage. But Jesus showed him that his morality and standing in the community wouldn't help him when he stood before a holy God. He had to be *born again*, out of Adam's sinful family into the righteous family of God.

We are *born again* when we become identified with Jesus through salvation. His righteousness is freely given to us, and our sin is cast away from us as far as the east is from the west. And remember, Dad, this is still true even on your worst day. This is also true for your children who know Christ, even on their worst days.

Taking in all we have talked about, we can confidently say that if our kids belong to Christ then we can know where their true identities lie. We can know because of the Holy Spirit's presence in them as His "temple" that there *will* be a desire to be obedient to God. In fact, God's Spirit *in* them is always 100 percent obedient to God. But their flesh is always 100 percent rebellious *toward* God.

If your children belong to God through a relationship with Christ, they can choose to walk in the Spirit or walk in the flesh.

You and I can do the same. But no matter what, the presence of God's Spirit in us makes us perfect, even as we struggle in our flesh with sin.

Parents are the primary disciple makers in their children's lives. As fathers, we want to make sure we are teaching them to acknowledge their own flesh patterns and surrender them to God.

"So I say, let the Holy Spirit guide your lives. Then you won't be doing what your sinful nature craves" (Gal. 5:16).

M46 Dads Challenge Four

Dad, are you clearly communicating the transformational gospel to your kids? Or are you giving them a dead, transactional religion that will eventually leave them disillusioned with Him? You can give your kids only what you yourself have. So it's very important that your own spiritual life is thriving.

Speaking age-appropriately, talk to your kids about baggage in your own life that has made things difficult for you to live out the truth of the gospel. Summarize in your own words what you have learned in this chapter. Teaching your children scriptural truths will also help reinforce them in your own life.

Talk to your kids about how the Bible teaches we are holy, perfect, and blameless in Christ even though we still struggle with sinful thoughts and behaviors. Make sure they understand that their own journeys of sanctification are about *progress, not perfection.*

Here is Jesus' prayer before He went to the cross. Imagine that He was talking about your own family, because He was.

> I am praying not only for these disciples but also for all who will ever believe in me through their message. I pray that they will all be one, just as you and I are one—as you are in me, Father, and I am in you. And may they be in us so that the world will believe you sent me.
>
> I have given them the glory you gave me, so they may be one as we are one. I am in them and you are in me. May they experience such perfect

unity that the world will know that you sent me and that you love them as much as you love me. Father, I want these whom you have given me to be with me where I am. Then they can see all the glory you gave me because you loved me even before the world began!

O righteous Father, the world doesn't know you, but I do; and these disciples know you sent me. I have revealed you to them, and I will continue to do so. Then your love for me will be in them, and I will be in them. (John 17:20–26)

Fight for the hearts of your children!

Les's M46 Moment

The Gospel of Grace

Grace is the best word I can use to describe my journey to Christ. I lived in darkness for thirty years and indulged myself in everything this world had to offer. Yet I could *never* fill the void inside my soul.

But all of that changed on March 3, 1993, in room 333 at the Best Western Hotel in Pittsburgh, Pennsylvania. I had what people in the church call a "Damascus road experience" from Jesus. What happened to me that night was a miracle as God's irresistible grace drew me to Him. I got radically saved, and the Lord then began to consume my life, transforming me forever.

A vivid M46 Moment for me was when I shared about my past with my son. I laid out the things I had experienced and the mistakes I'd made in my life. I also told him about the pain and guilt associated with it all.

While I felt I needed to communicate my full testimony with him, I was afraid he might think less of me or lose respect for me. But God actually used my vulnerability to allow us to begin to have deeper conversations and grow closer. Of course, my goal, besides being transparent with my son, was to help him avoid the traps that a young man can fall into.

I am very grateful for that M46 Challenge, because it created such a special time between my son and me, and it created a new openness in our relationship.

I want to set the example for my son by leading with authenticity and sharing with transparency. I want him to know that our Savior is not impressed with what we can do for Him, but rather He loves it when we simply acknowledge and rest in what He has done for us—to trust in His sufficiency for our lives, not in our own self-sufficiency.

I love that M46 Dads is about the gospel, the great news of Jesus Christ that can open our eyes and draw us in to hear the stories of other men who struggle with guilt, insecurities, fear, and understanding how Jesus' death on the cross has covered us all as children of God.

I love that M46 Dads is about the gospel, the great news of Jesus Christ that can open our eyes.

I feel privileged to be part of this ministry to dads across the world. I invite you to allow the Holy Spirit to reveal the truths you find in this book and let them penetrate your heart. Join us in this Rhino Revolution to lock arms and fight for the hearts of our children!

Chapter 5

Love, Acceptance, Worth, and Security

Dad, do you ever wonder why your kids make the choices they do? Why they choose the friends they do? Talk the way they do? Dress the way they do?

- Have you ever asked yourself those same questions?
- What drives us to act, think, and feel things we know are not wise and are sometimes even destructive?
- How can you help your kids recognize what is actually driving their decisions?
- What if you could help them see their own patterns long before they made any bad decisions?

Imagine your children being able to walk into *any* environment with any kind of peer pressure and know they have the personal tools to help them navigate through anything.

Imagine your children being able to walk
into *any* environment with any kind of peer
pressure and know they have the personal
tools to help them navigate through anything.

An unchanging truth in the Christian life is that you cannot lead anyone further than where you are. For that reason, you have to be willing to surrender your own life in this area before you can effectively pass the truth along to your children. Regardless of your family history or background, today's message can change an entire family legacy from this point forward, starting with you.

FREEDOM AND FULFILLMENT

What if your children could *know* they are complete just as they are? When the temptation to fit in and be accepted comes along, they can stand strong in their own identity. That ability is called *freedom*, a freedom that can come from only one Source.

Years ago, I (Tim) went through a counselor-training course at Grace Ministries International (GMI) in Marietta, Georgia, a disciple-making ministry that offers counseling, training, workshops, and conferences. Pastors from all over the world turn to Grace to become better-equipped disciplers.

I stumbled into GMI looking for answers but ended up going through about three years of counselor training myself. I soon realized God was doing something in me that He eventually would use to help others. Kind of like when the airlines tell you to put on your own oxygen mask before assisting others.

I will never forget the first time I heard Scott Brittin of GMI teach what I'm about to tell you. Everything changed when I saw him write this on the whiteboard in his office. I knew God was using this simple teaching to hold a mirror up in front of me to gently reveal *why* I had become *who* I had become. Issues were painfully exposed in me that, for some reason, I had never seen before.

That's the backstory. Since then, I have shared this truth with countless people. God's design for our basic needs is broken down into four categories, presented in the acronym L.A.W.S.:

L—love
A—acceptance
W—worth
S—security

Sharing this simple truth with your children as soon as they are able to understand the concept will make them aware of what is going on inside their hearts. As they get older, it can also help them have patience, empathy, and understanding as they deal with other people.

Here's what the teaching means: God designed us to have our needs of love, acceptance, worth, and security met only by, in, and through Jesus Christ. "Jesus answered, 'I am the way and the truth and the life. No one comes to the Father except through me'" (John 14:6 NIV).

We all go through life trying to get our needs met, mostly through relationships and material possessions. For example, we buy things we don't need or can't afford, all in an effort to impress people we say we don't care about. Some may look to substance abuse or other addictions to give them a sense of security. We can spend our lives trying to complete ourselves doing whatever it takes to find L.A.W.S.

We can even demand that other people approve, affirm, or complete us. But the truth is that no one has been created with the ability to fully do that. That strategy never works.

We can also just stand by and watch our children grow up and make their choices based on these same motivations from their own peer groups' expectations.

A person born into sin is separated from God and therefore has no access to Him apart from a relationship with Jesus. Some people who are right with God through salvation still do not understand that all of their needs are already met in Christ. One definition of sin might be when someone reaches for things other than Jesus to meet these internal needs.

The word *sanctification* is how we talk about the process in which God transforms people into the image of Jesus. Sanctification is God making His children more and more aware that they are complete in Christ and no longer need to look outside of Him to get their needs met.

TRADING THE OLD FOR THE NEW

In the context of this chapter, our definition of sin is *trying to get our needs met apart from Christ.* But in and through a covenant relationship with God through Christ, we don't have to reach for sinful substitutes to try to meet needs that He has already met.

> Yes, Adam's one sin brings condemnation for everyone, but Christ's one act of righteousness brings a right relationship with God and new life for everyone. Because one person disobeyed God, many became sinners. But because one other person obeyed God, many will be made righteous. (Rom. 5:18–19)

Even in our battles to meet our own needs and reach for wrong things outside of Christ, we are still made holy, perfect, and blameless in, by, and through His grace and mercy.

This is the gospel: our right standing with God is not based on our ever-flawed actions but rather the perfect performance of Jesus. We have the capability in Him to recognize our own patterns of the flesh and keep them from dragging us down a path toward sinful and destructive behavior. When those haunting temptations come along, we can stand on the truth that we are complete in Christ, no longer needing to reach for the old things to try to find life. That is true freedom.

"This means that anyone who belongs to Christ has become a new person. The old life is gone; a new life has begun!" (2 Cor. 5:17).

When we attempt to meet our needs apart from Christ, we spend a lot of time trying to show people who we *wish* we could be. We can work so hard to present a polished image of ourselves in the hopes that people will find us more appealing, attractive, successful, or impressive.

The word *hypocrite* can mean "a person who puts on a false appearance of virtue or religion."[6] Originally, the Greek word *hupokritēs* referred to an actor who wore a mask to hide his true identity. As far back as the first century, stage actors wore masks to play any role. These thespians were called "hypocrites," hence our modern-day word for people who try to portray to be someone they are not.

We can all be guilty of putting on a mask to get the sale, the job, the relationship, the respect we desire, or the admiration we seek. We try to present ourselves as cooler, less insecure, and far more confident than we actually are. So many people feel the need to create an alternative persona to hide what might be perceived as inferior. This is because we view brokenness as weakness.

Dad, our daughters are constantly trying to have one simple question answered: "Am I desirable?" They can obsess over their hair, appearance, and weight, driven by the fear they will be rejected and not find acceptance. Our sons are constantly asking of the world around them, "Do I have what it takes?" As dads, we do *not* want other people answering those questions for our daughters or sons, because the answers they find there will most likely be false and harmful.

Today, every aspect of our culture and the media focuses on our differences and how they make each of us "special." Everyone is trying to figure out a way to stand out from everybody else. But looking at the human heart and soul, we all need the same things. We love the same and we hurt in the same ways from the same root issues.

Our kids will often take part in risky and dangerous behavior just to prove themselves to their peers to try to meet their internal needs. Our responsibility is to answer the questions our sons and daughters ask from deep inside their hearts so they will feel less compelled to look for those solutions from anyone or anything besides Christ and their identities as children of God. A major part of our job is to show them this is true, regardless of their ever-changing feelings.

The bottom line: resting in the finished work of Jesus is essential both in understanding our identity and in learning to live a life of real freedom.

RADICAL REALIZATION

In John chapter 4, we see how Jesus interacted with a Samaritan woman He met at a water well. Due to cultural racism, Jews did not associate with Samaritans. Also, Jewish men did not speak to women in public. But as usual, Jesus blew past all of man's boundaries and talked with this Samaritan woman about her life.

> She said to Jesus, "You are a Jew, and I am a Samaritan woman. Why are you asking me for a drink?"
>
> Jesus replied, "If you only knew the gift God has for you and who you are speaking to, you would ask me, and I would give you living water." (John 4:9–10)

Thinking that Jesus was referring to the water in the well, she asked Him to explain how His water could possibly be better.

> Jesus replied, "Anyone who drinks this water will soon become thirsty again. But those who drink the water I give will never be thirsty again. It becomes a fresh, bubbling spring within them, giving them eternal life."

> "Please, sir," the woman said, "give me this
> water! Then I'll never be thirsty again, and I won't
> have to come here to get water." (John 4:13–15)

Jesus was trying to teach the woman that her L.A.W.S.—love, acceptance, worth, and security—could be met only in Him, not in the five husbands she'd had or the man she was living with at the time. What she had found with each of those relationships was that they could not deliver what she had reached out for time and again. But suddenly, she understood what Christ was telling her: she had *eternal* needs that Jesus *needed* to meet, but she also had *internal* needs that He *wanted* to meet.

> The woman left her water jar beside the well and
> ran back to the village, telling everyone, "Come and
> see a man who told me everything I ever did! Could
> he possibly be the Messiah?" (John 4:28–29)

In that simple encounter, Jesus forever changed her life. As this woman found, understanding what Christ is to us can revolutionize our lives.

One thing I have learned about God and understanding His truths is that it's never too late to change—as a man and as a dad. He is always restoring and constantly reconciling. The more you can grasp that God has a covenant love for you and that the finished work of His Son has removed all the obstacles between you and Him, the more you can communicate this truth to your kids.

The bottom-line truth we have to receive for ourselves and teach our children is that if we go to God for our needs, we can truly find contentment. But if we go to the world for our needs, we will just remain thirsty.

I never really understood John 10:10, when Jesus shared about abundant life. But I finally realized He was talking about real, authentic contentment, the kind the world cannot give. No matter our external circumstances, if we are content in our hearts, we can be satisfied. That's all any of us really needs, and all that we seek. No more will our lives be about settling but rather about finding real life in Christ.

Now that we are halfway through the book, we hope you are beginning to understand that being a better dad is not so much about getting the correct parental advice—more dos and don'ts—but being certain the gospel is truly transforming your heart so you can be earthly evidence of Jesus to your kids.

Being a better dad is not so much about getting the correct parental advice—more dos and don'ts—but being certain the gospel is truly transforming your heart so you can be earthly evidence of Jesus to your kids.

Please remember, Dad, *you* are the most influential man in the life of your children. You alone have the opportunity to share the truths of the gospel with your kids that will lead them to the True Well of Living Water where they will never thirst again.

M46 Dads Challenge Five

Talk to your kids about how you have tried to find love, acceptance, worth, and security apart from God. Be transparent, but share appropriately.

Then ask them if they recognize any of their own patterns.

Talk to them about their identities in Christ.

Promise your kids that you are always available to listen to them and help them find how their needs can be met in Jesus.

Fight for the hearts of your children!

Robbie's M46 Moment

Father's Sacrifice

I am the proud dad of three young ladies whom I love with all my heart. When M46 Dads began, my daughters were teenagers. As I went to our CRASH meetings, I started to realize so many things I could have done better and could still improve on as a father. One major dynamic I took to heart in our challenges was being intentional as a dad.

I had always worked hard to be present at all my girls' activities. I once drove two and a half hours to watch a three-minute play. We prayed every morning when we got in the car before we left for school. Every Wednesday morning when the girls were in high school, we had breakfast as a family at Chick-fil-A. Those are just some of the ways I was intentional as a dad, but there were many ways I failed.

When my oldest daughter turned twenty-one, I reflected over the years and how I had come to better understand God's love for me through His intentional love, grace, and sacrifice as a Father. When she was born and I held her for the first time, I could not believe how much I already loved her. And yet I did not know her. Then I was reminded that God sent His Son to a sinful place to die for a disgusting person like me. I cannot comprehend how Someone could give His child for me. But God did.

I also began to understand grace as my daughter grew up. She, like us all, has made mistakes, lied, disobeyed, and been disrespectful to us as her parents. But that *never* affected my love for her. She is my daughter, and no matter what her actions were, my love for her never changed.

Our sacrifices showed me how much my own parents did for me as a child and still do today. As parents, we sacrifice daily for our children, and they will not understand how much … until they become parents themselves.

The pain that God must have felt as He saw His Son hanging on the cross is incomprehensible to me as a father. The pain I have experienced through the tough decisions and mistakes our girls have made, and how hard it was when my oldest daughter went away to college, has made me realize the pain I must have caused my own parents. Through my time at M46 Dads, I forgave my own dad for his failures.

Through my time at M46 Dads, I forgave my own dad for his failures.

I want to keep being challenged to be intentional and even to make up now for past failures. But the truth is that, as much as we strive to be the best dads we can be, we are also guaranteed to fail sometimes. But no matter what, I am so proud to have the name "Dad," even with all the sacrifices.

Part Two

FAMILY

Chapter 6

The Four Dads

In the 1920s, Dr. Evan Kane, a chief surgeon, faced a difficult dilemma. Many of his patients could not receive the basic surgeries they desperately needed, because at that time, only general anesthesia was used, which put patients to sleep. For those with heart conditions and similar issues, this was considered too dangerous. However, Dr. Kane had a theory that local anesthesia could be used for minor surgeries. If the patient didn't have to be put completely under, many more people could be helped. But no one had ever tried this approach.

Dr. Kane attempted to find a volunteer upon whom to do an actual surgery with local anesthesia only, but as you can imagine, there were no takers. So on February 15, 1921, the good doctor successfully performed an appendectomy surgery on *himself.*[7]

Now *that*, my friend, is total commitment—100 percent all in. Cutting your own incision, sacrificing yourself, and risking the pain for the greater good.

But, Dad, very often that is exactly what we must do for the greater good of our families. Throughout this chapter, I (Kenny) am going to ask you to perform some spiritual surgery on yourself.

To commit to being an M46 Dad, let's start by examining two areas: dealing with our own fathers' influence and taking responsibility for our own issues.

TAKING OWNERSHIP FOR OUR STUFF

No matter our relationships with our dads, we have to honestly address what we inherited from them and what we will choose to change. A child is a victim of circumstances with little or no choice, but an adult man has the freedom to choose his own path. Blaming Dad for the past does not excuse our current sins, nor does it have to define our future.

No matter our relationships with our dads, we have to honestly address what we inherited from them and what we will choose to change.

There is a term that professional counselors use to describe any sort of pain that has been inflicted by a dad: *father-wound*. Because we were all raised by sinners, we all have some sort of wound or wounds. The choice is what we will do with them.

If our fathers have hurt us, we will take one of two paths: repeat or repent.

- Repeat: We will carry on the same sins and unhealthy patterns we experienced as kids. The cycle will continue and be passed to the next generation in our parenting.
- Repent: We will surrender our lives fully to Christ and turn from the sin, patterns, and bad habits

of our families. We will change the course of our
parenting and model God's will, ways, and Word.

The second thing we have to do to commit to being an M46 Dad
involves facing our own issues, taking full responsibility for our parenting, and looking to God for His leadership.

Just the fact that we carry wounds from our relationships with our
own dads, coupled with our own fears and concerns, causes most of us
to truly work hard as fathers. Yet this harsh reality can also make us feel
the weight of not being equipped to be the dads we really want to be.

Our views of our fathers profoundly affect our views of God, which
in turn dramatically impact the way we parent our children. As Tim
shared in an earlier chapter, we as dads are painting a picture of God for
our children. We bring into our own families the parenting paradigm
we witnessed and experienced from our dads and moms. We can give
only what we have.

Here are a couple of key questions about your relationship growing
up with your father. Write your answers in the blanks or in a journal.

How would you describe your father?

How would you describe your relationship with your father, growing
up?

As we move forward, keep your answers in mind. Later, we will reflect back on how similar *or* how different your relationship is with your children. Regardless, be open to what the Lord will reveal to you in this chapter. Please remember—in everything we communicate in this book, the goal is grace, not grief. The goal is conviction from God, not condemnation.

Next, we're going to offer you a powerful resource we call "The Four Dads" that will allow you to determine where you stand among four different types of fathers, four distinct parenting styles.

Take a moment to look at the following graphic, and then continue reading. You'll be using this for the rest of the chapter and in your challenge.

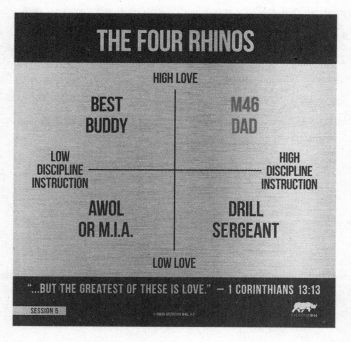

LOVE AND INSTRUCTION

The axis with "High Love" at the top and "Low Love" at the bottom is designed to graph your love for your children. High love is the covenant, unconditional love that Tim talked about earlier. The very top of this line is God's unconditional love. Low love would be apathetic and lazy at best, with abuse, neglect, or abandonment at worst. The end of the line could even be described as "No Love."

The horizontal axis, with "High Discipline/Instruction" on the right and "Low Discipline/Instruction" on the left, is designed to graph your level of discipline and instruction. Think of discipline as defense and instruction as offense. A team must have both to be strong and win. High discipline/instruction means being crystal clear about right and wrong, focused on teaching the best way to live. Low discipline/instruction means there is no direction provided at all. The end on this line is zero supervision.

We know you can be all over this chart at different times in your parenting. What we're after here is to find where you typically land in a daily context. Using these two components, we can get good readings on our parenting styles.

Take a moment to look at the "Love" line. Taking your time to be fair but honest with yourself, draw a dot on the line where you believe it best represents how you parent day to day.

Next, look at the "Discipline/Instruction" line. Draw a dot on the line where you believe it best represents how you parent day to day.

Last, draw a line connecting your two dots. When you are done, the line should form a triangle in one of the four quadrants.

- Top-left quadrant—high love and low discipline/ instruction: This is the "Best Buddy Dad," a permissive father who just wants to be buddies with his kids. This father definitely shows love to his child, but he does not use his influence and authority to provide sufficient guidance or instruction. He constantly answers "Sure, you know it's fine with me, but you better go ask your mom" to avoid any conflict and to transfer his responsibility. We all know people who were spoiled through their entire childhood. There is a strong likelihood they had Best Buddy Dads. The end result of behavior from these kids can range from a lack of self-discipline to full-blown entitlement.

- Bottom-left quadrant—low love and low discipline/instruction: This is the "Mr. AWOL Dad." The reality of this parent is neglect—AWOL (absent without leave). He either has completely abandoned his child by being physically absent or is present in his child's life but is emotionally unavailable and relationally invisible. This dad may even live in the same house, but his child does not feel a relationship is available in any manner. The effects on a child can range from total disregard and disrespect for authority to being completely passive, fearful, and insecure.

- Bottom-right quadrant—high discipline/instruction and low love: This is the "Drill Sergeant Dad." The Drill Sergeant Dad is driven by rules, regulations, and intense instruction. Life is very black and white, and total, unchallenged obedience is the only acceptable answer. While this father clearly states the difference between right and wrong, very little love is ever communicated. Life under his roof is lived under law, and the joy in this relationship between the father and his child is lacking. There is no question who is in charge, and the environment is managed by fear and control.

- Top-right quadrant—high discipline/instruction and high love: This is the "M46 Dad," a father who clearly teaches his child right from wrong and does so in a loving relationship. He is not perfect, and he makes his share of mistakes, but his child doesn't question his love in the process. Life under his roof is lived under God's grace.

PERCEPTION IS REALITY

We hope this exercise has given you a clearer picture of your style of parenting. But here's a plot twist for you: where *you* believe you stand on this graph doesn't actually matter.

The only thing that truly matters is where your children perceive you to be.

And each one of your children will have his or her own individual perception based on variables such as age, birth order, gender, and level of relationship.

Let me give you an example of how perceptions can be very different. My (Kenny's) children once attended a school that required them to wear a specific shoe that cost $70. At that time, the rule in my house was that *no one* gets more than $40 for a pair of shoes. So when I broke down and laid out the $70 for my kindergartner's shoes, you better believe I knew 100 percent that I loved my kid.

But guess what? My kindergartner didn't know that I loved him just because I bought him a $70 pair of shoes. That's not something a child would likely be able to understand. I might have thought I'd showed a lot of love, but in my child's eyes, "love" would have been if I'd given him candy instead of expensive shoes.

Ask yourself the tough question of where your individual children would place you on this graph. Not where *you* would place yourself. Using our Dr. Kane analogy, commit to some self-surgery.

If you really want to know the answer to that question, you're going to have to let them plot you on the graph themselves.

- Draw out the Four Rhinos graph on a piece of paper (a new graph for each child).
- Explain very simply what each term means.
- Explain what the lines represent.
- Assure that there will be no consequences for their honesty with you.
- Be certain your child understands how to use the graph.

- Leave your child alone for a few minutes to circle their dots and draw their lines.
- When your child is done, thank and reassure him or her.

Buckle up, Dad. This exercise can be very affirming or very painful. And sometimes, depending on how many kids you have, possibly both. Don't take anything personally or get hurt, as tough as that might be. This is the time to have rhino hide. Take any potentially negative evaluation and use it for fuel to become an M46 Dad. Let the truth set you free to be all that God wants you to be as a father.

FOLLOW-UP FROM THE FOUR DADS EXERCISE

Well, which sort of dad do your kids say you are?

Are you the Best Buddy Dad, who needs his children to like him above anything else? Who is that about—you or the kids?

Are you the Mr. AWOL Dad, who gets so caught up in his work, hobbies, life, and issues that time passes and he is absent in some way? Who is that about—you or the kids?

Are you the Drill Sergeant Dad, who just wants things to go right and smooth for him? Who is that about—you or the kids?

A WORD TO MY FELLOW DRILL SERGEANT DADS

So many of us today work long hours "for the family." This means we often come through the door exhausted, ready for peace and quiet at the end of the day. But this is dad prime time for our kids! When they are young, they are so excited to see their daddy. We must be extremely careful to make sure that even when we are tired, we aren't just barking out orders to everyone, "Get your homework done! Get ready for bed! Be quiet!"

The Drill Sergeant Dad approach doesn't produce what we might expect in the life of his kid. That is exactly the way the gospel and the law work. The law doesn't produce what we think it will produce. Only the gospel can create a heart for God. All the law can create is the fearful expectation of judgment.

The parenting style that is statistically most likely to create a rebellious child is the Drill Sergeant. Why? Have you ever worked for a boss who couldn't care less about you? Did you ever have a class with a teacher who you knew did not care anything about you or whether or not you learned the material? Were you motivated to love that class or job, or did you dread going?

Dad, the Drill Sergeant style of parenting may get results for a few years when the children are young. But that approach is a ticking time bomb that you have personally set for the detonation of the relationship. As soon as the child is old enough, the rebellion begins. The big surprise for the Drill Sergeant is that he thinks everything is under his thumb until ... boom! One day, everything blows up and then the challenge is to pick up the pieces.

Dad, your children need your godly discipline, vision, and instruction. But they also need your love. I once heard parenting described this way: Our children are like a fast-flowing river. The discipline and instruction we provide give them high banks to keep them flowing in the right direction. If the banks get soft and washed out, the river floods in all directions, bringing chaos.

THE M46 DAD—BEING INTENTIONAL

So how do you become an M46 Dad? After all, godly fatherhood doesn't happen by accident.

Be intentional in spending time with your children. Show love in both quantity and quality, while also rightly and fairly disciplining and instructing. For most dads, this time is a few hours in the evenings with dedicated blocks on the weekends, possibly around household chores and precious personal time.

But an M46 Dad views *every* moment with his children as sacred time. Intentional time can be pushing them on a swing or helping with homework, watching a movie together or talking about a problem at school, playing in the yard or reading a Bible story at bedtime. Do things that *your children* love, and do them with your full attention.

Do things that *your children* love, and do them with your full attention.

Be intentional in communication with your children. Have dinner at the table with no electronics present. Designate device-free times and device-free zones. Encourage real conversation by asking questions about their day and their lives. Starting this practice when they are young can set a pattern for when they get older.

Be intentional in talking about God with your children. Talk to your children about God, and pray with them as they go to bed each night. Share openly and honestly about your own experiences with God to let them see how He is a part of your life and how you have a real relationship with Him. That dynamic will be like a magnet drawing your kids to Christ.

Be intentional with your personal attention. Schedule times and activities where you focus 100 percent on your children—together and individually. No phone. No tablet. No calls. No emails. No texts. No distractions. If everyone who is truly important to you is in the room, what call, text, or game score should you let take priority over your family? When your kids are little, if they see your phone taking precedence over them, when they get to be teenagers, they'll return the same behavior to you.

Be intentional with your love for your children. Express love for your children verbally, physically, and regularly. Your children must know your love for them is never dependent on what they say or do and that nothing will ever change that fact. As their dad, you can simply reflect the beautiful covenant love to your children that Christ has already freely given to you.

I like this family slogan: "Rules without Relationship equals Rebellion." But let's add the other extreme: "Relationship with no Rules equals Running (all over you)." The biblical balance of the M46 Dad is "Relationship with the Right Rules equals Righteousness."

LOVE OF A FATHER

First Corinthians 13 is the famous "love chapter" in the Bible. Here's a version adapted to express a father's commitment of godly love for his children. Use this as both a prayer to God and a declaration to your kids:

> As a dad, I will be patient and kind. I will not show envy, boasting, or pride to my kids. I will not dishonor them by being self-seeking. I won't be easily angered by them and I won't keep a record of their wrongs. As a dad, I won't cooperate with evil but I will rejoice in the truth. As a dad, I will always protect, always trust, always hope, always persevere for my kids. I vow my love will never fail them. I will be the man my kids need to see and put my own childish ways behind me. I want my kids to fully know God through me, even as I am fully known. And now these three remain for me as their dad: faith, hope, and love. But the greatest of these is love. (Adapted from 1 Cor. 13:4–8, 11–13 NIV)

God gave the children of Israel an incredible charge regarding His Word and His ways. This passage integrates the entire family and everyday life, perfectly applying to us today.

> And you must love the LORD your God with all your heart, all your soul, and all your strength. And you must commit yourselves wholeheartedly to these commands that I am giving you today. Repeat them again and again to your children. Talk about them when you are at home and when you are on

the road, when you are going to bed and when you are getting up. Tie them to your hands and wear them on your forehead as reminders. Write them on the doorposts of your house and on your gates. (Deut. 6:5–9)

M46 Dads Challenge Six

Dad, your challenge in this chapter is to take your kids through the Four Dads quadrant exercise found in the "Perception Is Reality" section several pages back. Follow the instructions we have offered you there.

Pray before you engage with your children, and ask for God's leadership and blessing over this crucial time for your family.

When you are evaluating your kids' graphs, prayerfully decide how you can give your intentional attention to change any attitudes or actions reflected in how your kids see you.

Fight for the hearts of your children!

Quincy's M46 Moment

The Art of Listening

I have been blessed to be a part of M46 Dads since the beginning. The lessons I have learned during our sessions have helped improve my relationship with my four kids and my beautiful wife.

When I was eight, my dad left with no notice and never came back. My mom later remarried, but my stepdad was never involved in our lives. The only thing I remember about him was one time at the dinner table when he got upset because I didn't eat my green beans. He proceeded to tell me how my life would not amount to "three cents" and I would *never* succeed.

That story sums up how I was raised. Not eating green beans meant my life would be worthless.

But as I look back, ironically, that became a defining moment for me. I decided I would prove to my stepdad that I not only *could* succeed but *would* succeed. However, that drive would eventually have a profound negative effect on my relationship with my own kids.

I focused all my energy into my career rather than my family. I worked relentlessly to bring in enough wealth to prove I was worth more than three cents. I didn't see that my plan backfired— because I was giving my family only three cents' worth of love and attention.

Every M46 Dads session left us with a challenge to assess our relationships and ask our kids some hard questions. Each time, I learned how to build an intentional relationship with my kids. Before, my focus had always been my work. Now when I was with my family, I concentrated on making sure they knew I was focused on them! At least, I thought that was the case.

When we did the Four Dads session, I just knew that challenge was bound to be an easy discussion with my kids. This was going to be a slam dunk because of how involved I'd become in their lives. After dinner that night, I plotted out the graph and explained the quadrants to my four kids. Then I had each of them do their own.

I knew for three of my kids, I would likely still be somewhere in the Drill Sergeant zone. But I just felt that one son would definitely call me an M46 Dad. For the past six months, I had been coaching him in football. And we spent three days a week talking during our car rides to and from practice. On Saturdays, since he was on a travel football team, we would spend six to eight hours together. He and I were racking up a lot of time.

When my kids finished their graphs, I noticed that this son did not want me to see his result. Finally, he leaned into his mother and began to cry. He said he didn't want to share what he had put on his paper. I explained that whatever he drew would not matter and was going to help me grow as a father. Once again, I was thinking there was no way I was not the perfect dad in his eyes. *Maybe the joy of him telling me was making him cry?* But I was so wrong.

When he finally surrendered his graph, I saw he had labeled me as an AWOL Dad.

I immediately launched into defense mode. How could I be *absent* in his life? But then I saw how much he was hurting. He told me that for the past six months I had been there but never took the time to ask what *he* wanted to talk about. I had just always talked about football.

In that tough moment, I learned that being a part of my kids' lives is always more than just being there physically. I had to learn to serve my kids by *really* listening to them, by truly being present.

I had to learn to serve my kids by *really* listening to them, by truly being present.

Chapter 7

The Cup

Let's review some of the topics we've introduced. The goal is for these concepts to become second nature in your thinking so you can share them often with your children as they grow and mature. Then we're going to look at these truths through a practical lens and talk about how to pass them on to your kids.

Recall the L.A.W.S. acronym of man's four basic needs:

- L—love
- A—acceptance
- W—worth
- S—security

God created us to have these four needs met only in, through, and by Him. When someone is not in a relationship with Christ, he will seek out substitutes that cannot and will not satisfy these needs. Even so, there are many people who claim to be Christ-followers yet simply do not understand these four qualities are available *now*, in the person of Jesus in us.

I (Tim) want to remind you of the definition of sin we previously shared. Sin is trying to get any or all of these needs met apart from God.

The bottom line is that either we will allow a relationship with Jesus to meet these four needs or we will try anyone and everything else to have them met somewhere, somehow, someway. My story illustrated how I believed in Jesus but had no idea how to allow Him to meet my deepest needs. I had to hit bottom to finally look to Him and not to myself, others, or even the church.

Either we will allow a relationship with Jesus to meet these four needs or we will try anyone and everything else to have them met somewhere, somehow, someway.

Granted, we don't always *feel* like our needs are met in Christ. We don't always *feel* complete or full in Him, because our flesh gets in the way. But part of the journey of sanctification is learning to trust the *fact* that our needs are already met. We are continually learning and expressing faith that we don't have to reach outside of Him to find love, acceptance, worth, and security.

Since dads cannot give away what they do not have, we must continually ask ourselves:

- *How* am I trying to get my needs met apart from Jesus?
- *Where* am I trying to get my needs met apart from Jesus?
- *From whom* am I trying to get my needs met apart from Jesus?
- *Why* am I trying to get my needs met apart from Jesus?

Some other important questions:

- Am I in crushing debt because of the things I've bought for appearance's sake?
- Am I obsessed with my bank account or investments?
- Does my security come from money or power?
- Am I draining the life from my wife out of unrealistic demands and expectations?
- Am I driven by other people's perceptions?
- Am I constantly trying to show people who I wish I could be, rather than who I actually am?
- Do I fear I am risking too much if someone knows who I truly am?

And then if the answer to any of these is yes, we must look deep inside our hearts to ask, "Why?"

Left unchecked, these areas will always eventually manifest in the physical realm. But they all begin as identity issues and perceived unmet needs in our hearts. Early on, issues are typically not visible, but as they progress, they slowly grow deep inside or we begin to operate in secret to meet our own needs.

Here are some overarching personal questions that reflect the L.A.W.S. needs:

- When I feel unloved, I tend to go to _____.
- When I feel unaccepted, I tend to go to _____.
- When I feel unworthy, I tend to go to _____.
- When I feel insecure, I tend to go to _____.
- When I feel ashamed, I tend to go to _____.
- When I feel I've been treated unfairly, I tend to go to _____.
- When I feel inferior, I tend to go to _____.

Asking these questions for an honest evaluation can save us a great deal of trouble and pain later. These personal questions are not meant to create any guilt or shame but to help you be a healthy, mature, and Christlike M46 Dad.

With the L.A.W.S. acronym as the foundation, let's build some walls of protection for your kids by providing you with another practical tool to help them experience freedom in Christ.

THE POINT OF PARENTING

Dad, God created your kids with these same four basic needs. Your daughter is walking through life seeking them. Your son is driven to meet them. They are asking the world: *Am I desirable? Am I lovable? Am I enough? Do I have what it takes to make it in this world?*

We can certainly help them and reinforce the answers to these questions for our kids. But the biggest and best effort we can make is to point them to Jesus to be the One to define them and meet their needs. We have the awesome responsibility to help them see the true Source for their answers, where real life is found, and where their identity comes from.

We do not want our daughters and sons out there looking for love, acceptance, worth, and security apart from God. If they are still starving for acceptance when they reach middle school, what might they be willing to do to get it? Especially as their freedom to choose expands outside the safe boundaries of our homes.

This is yet another reason for us as dads to be aware of our *own* tendencies to reach for things outside of Jesus for validation. We can be more alert and sensitive to our *kids'* tendencies. An old proverb says: What parents do in moderation, children may do in excess.

Imagine an empty cup in your hand, in your daughter's hand, or in your son's hand. No one can see this cup, but we all walk around with it held out in front of us. Anyone who does not have a relationship with Jesus is constantly looking to have their cup filled. They try anything and everything they can find, but every solution ultimately fails.

How is it, then, that Christians can sometimes behave in the same way? As Christ-followers, unless we know our cup is already full, we are also going to be looking for how, where, and when to get it filled and who will fill it.

Many years ago, I was crushed by a Christian friend with whom I was very close. When we are wronged as Christ-followers, we know what we are supposed to do, right? We are clearly told in the Bible how to respond. We are called to forgive. That's Christianity 101.

So I gathered my thoughts and took this person to lunch. I reached across the table, so to speak, as far as I could. But this person never acknowledged what they had done. But I verbally forgave them anyway, as I knew I should. I thought I'd been the model of Christian forgiveness.

I soon began to notice that every single time I was around the person, I thought my heart was going to beat out of my chest. Before long, I realized I was not right with this person at all. The offense was still very much alive to me. My mouth had confessed forgiveness, but in my heart, I knew better.

Someone very wise once gave me a great definition of forgiveness. You truly forgive when you can say to the person who created the offense, "You don't owe me anything." If I was trying to make the other person admit guilt, I knew I hadn't truly allowed forgiveness.

I was holding that invisible cup out in front of me every time I was around that person. I was demanding in my heart, "Fill my cup back up, please. You took something from me. Now put it back." Forgiveness is choosing to put the cup down and profess, "You don't owe me *anything*."

And *why* can we say that? *How* can we say that? Because Christ has already filled our cup, so no person or circumstance on this earth can take that away or remove His filling. That also means that no person can put anything in our cup—or back in our cup—that will satisfy.

The M46 Dad knows he is already complete in Christ. That man knows who and Whose he is. He is not easily offended and does not demand respect. A great quote I once heard is, "You can't be spiritually mature and emotionally immature at the same time." Another is, "A man can gauge his spiritual maturity by the length of time between an offense toward him and his forgiveness of it."

The M46 Dad knows he is already complete in Christ.

I'm not discounting the damage that can be done through abuse, neglect, or abandonment. But as Christ-followers, we need to acknowledge that true forgiveness is always the goal.

THE CUP OF CHRIST

You have likely taken part in Communion or the Lord's Supper many times at church. You know well what the minister always states about the bread and the cup. But we want you to connect the cup we have talked about thus far to a major truth in Christ's teaching.

> And he took a cup of wine and gave thanks to God for it. He gave it to them and said, "Each of you drink from it, for this is my blood, which confirms the covenant between God and his people. It is poured out as a sacrifice to forgive the sins of many." (Matt. 26:27–28)

Here we have biblical evidence that our cup is filled by Christ alone. Recall what we've covered on the old and new covenants, especially how Christ passed through every barrier and satisfied all God's requirements to restore and redeem our sin. Now notice that the cup He used in this passage "confirms the covenant between God and his people." Christ's blood filled our cup. Taking part in Communion at church should be a constant reminder that our cup is full.

Lastly, when we truly believe and live knowing our cup is full, God can use us by pouring our lives into others. When we live in the truth that Christ has an endless supply of His qualities in us, we can give to others, knowing there is no limit to what He can do. The bottom line is that we cannot out-give God, and He replenishes anything that we give away in His name.

> Forgive others, and you will be forgiven. Give, and you will receive. Your gift will return to you in full—pressed down, shaken together to make room for more, running over, and poured into your lap. The amount you give will determine the amount you get back. (Luke 6:37–38)

Dad, we do not want our kids to walk around with their cups in their hands, begging or demanding that people, things, achievements, or circumstances make them feel whole. We want them to know who they are and Whose they are. Fight for the hearts of your children by teaching them that they are complete and full in Christ.

M46 Dads Challenge Seven

Dad, for this challenge, you need to give each of your kids a cup.

Take time to sit down to teach them about their spiritual cups. Talk them through how the things of this world will offer to fill their cups and how they will often feel like other things or relationships need to be in their cups.

Encourage them to come to you when they are struggling with feeling like their cups are empty or in need of something or someone else. This will open up dialogue opportunities between you and them. Make sure you don't shut them down when they're sharing their temptations. This practice could literally save their lives one day.

Tell them how you recognize that you sometimes hold your cup out for others. Give them an example from your own life of when you worked hard to get someone to approve of you, such as a boss or friend or someone you struggled to forgive.

Ask your kids how they see this play out in their own lives and where they are being tempted to hold out their cups.

Read them the Matthew 26 passage (or Mark 14 or Luke 22), and connect how Christ's sacrifice on the cross and resurrection made provision for their cups to be full forever.

Close by reminding them that if they are in Christ, their cups are full, they are not needy, and they are complete. Even when they don't *feel* it, the *fact* is that Jesus is *in* them if they *belong* to Him.

> For I want you to understand what really matters, so
> that you may live pure and blameless lives until the

day of Christ's return. May you always be filled with
the fruit of your salvation—the righteous character
produced in your life by Jesus Christ—for this will
bring much glory and praise to God. (Phil. 1:10–11)

Fight for the hearts of your children!

Mike's M46 Moment

Rekindled Hope

Any man can be a father. But to be a *good* father … that is the hardest thing I have ever done in my life.

What makes it so hard for me is that the thing I wanted most in this life was to *have* a good father. But by the time I was an adult, I began to strive for the approval of my dad by working to be excellent and successful at everything I did. And I became successful. I have been very blessed.

As my four children grew up, I wanted to be purposeful and deliberate in teaching them how to live and be successful too. Yet the reality was that, even though I was physically present at all their events and took the family on vacations to be a good dad, I was mentally and emotionally absent.

As I got involved with M46 Dads, I began to see what my baggage from my dad had created with my own kids. I started to realize that today, even though my children are in their twenties and out of college, it's *not* over … regardless of their age.

The main thing God helped me to realize was that I needed to just enjoy being in the presence of my kids. To just enjoy being with them, not doing *for* them. Just like God wants me to just enjoy being in His presence as His child.

M46 rekindled the hope for me as a dad that it is not over. It's not too late.

I want dads to know that it's okay if you have screwed up. It is never too late. Lighten up. Be at peace. Enjoy your kids. Like me, you can still invest in their lives. You can turn your heart to their hearts. You can lead them to God's heart.

It's okay if you have screwed up. Lighten up. Be at peace. Enjoy your kids. Like me, you can still invest in their lives.

Chapter 8

Encouragement vs. Exasperation

A few years ago, a news article about a four-year-old boy grabbed my (Kenny's) attention. The story was very sad and, unfortunately, far too common in our self-centered culture. Authorities were forced to remove the child from his home because his mother and father had been abusing him. When the officers asked the little boy, "What's your name?" he quietly answered, "Idiot."

He had been called an idiot so many times that he believed it was his actual name. Can you imagine the kind of pain and emotional baggage this child will have to deal with when he gets older? Consider the struggle he may have if he tries to understand the unconditional covenant love that his heavenly Father has for him.

You may have heard the old saying "Sticks and stones may break my bones, but words will never hurt me." We all know that phrase was just a clever comeback to put up a brave front, because words *definitely* hurt us. The Bible tells us what's true: "The words of the reckless pierce like swords" (Prov. 12:18 NIV).

Interesting how we use the term "cutting remarks" to describe when someone speaks mean and hateful words to us. We certainly understand the metaphor of how words pierce our hearts like swords, inflicting emotional pain.

A lot of dads in our culture feel that their bank account, social status, or education will be the greatest factor to help their children be successful. But the truth we cover in this chapter may be the single most crucial weapon in the dad arsenal. If you want to help your children be successful, *be careful with your words*. "The tongue has the power of life and death" (Prov. 18:21 NIV).

Our tongues make the difference between speaking encouragement and life to our kids and speaking exasperation and death to their spirits.

Take a moment to think about how you normally—day in and day out—speak to your children. Do they feel a tone and attitude of encouragement from you most of the time? Or do they feel the life being sucked out of them by your constant criticisms?

Asking these deeply personal questions is intended to help you see reality as a dad. If you find that something needs to be addressed, then you have the God-given grace to change what you are doing. Please keep that truth in mind as we move through this chapter.

COACH MODE

There is a verse that God speaks directly to each one of us as fathers: "Fathers, do not exasperate your children, so that they will not lose heart" (Col. 3:21 NASB). We think it should be meditated on and memorized as a constant reminder for us dads.

The word *exasperate* simply means "to provoke or ignite." Here are a few other translations or paraphrases to help us see the spirit of the verse:

- "Fathers, do not aggravate your children, or they will become discouraged" (NLT).
- "Fathers, do not nag your children. If you are too hard to please, they may want to stop trying" (NCV).
- "Fathers, provoke not your children, that they be not discouraged" (ASV).
- "Fathers, don't make your children resentful, or they will become discouraged" (GW).
- "Fathers, do not be so hard on your children that they will give up trying to do what is right" (NLV).
- "Parents, don't come down too hard on your children or you'll crush their spirits" (THE MESSAGE).

The Bible is full of if/then statements. This is yet another strong example. If a father exasperates, aggravates, nags, provokes, or comes down too hard on his kids, they could lose heart, become discouraged, stop trying, or have their spirits crushed. The New Life Version takes the outcome a step further: "They will give up trying to do what is right." Regardless of which version you read, this verse should be a wake-up call about the power of our words.

As a high school football coach for the last twenty-plus years, I yell, bark orders, call out quick decisions, and throw out constant feedback on how our playbook ought to be run and how performance can be improved. With a twenty-five-second play clock ticking, I am not given the luxury of time to explain myself, so I am forced to spew out the unfiltered facts and commands.

One of the mistakes I've made over the years is using that same approach at home. But no matter how hard I try to cut down on it, my family still experiences too much of that from me. In fact, they have named it "Coach Mode." I will say or do something, and one of my kids will call out to the rest of the family, "Dad's in Coach Mode!"

Busted … again.

My kids have been brutally honest and shared with me that I am not a well-loved man when I'm in Coach Mode at home. And when I speak and act that way, they certainly do not feel loved by me.

Being extremely busy as dads and also men dealing with our own flesh, we have to be very careful with our words. Without even thinking, and certainly without meaning to, we can so easily exasperate our kids. Not like the verbal, emotional, or physical abuse we saw in the "Idiot" story, but there are certainly ways we can suck the life out of our kids and crush their spirits without realizing what we have done.

And "fair" or not, God seems to have given dads a megaphone when it comes to their words and their kids. Truly, the tongue holds the power of life and death for our children.

Here are six "exasperators" we must watch out for in communication with our children:

- *Unrealistic Expectations:* We cannot communicate to our kids that our love is performance-based. As a coach, I see this all the time—performance directly connected to praise or criticism, with no in-between. Give more high fives at their victories than disappointed expressions at their losses.

- *Comparison to Peers:* We can be guilty of constantly comparing our children to other kids—or even worse, to a successful sibling. That rejection can be devastating and permanently damaging for them. Far too many adults grew up hearing their dads say, "Why can't you be more like your brother/sister?" That message creates serious divisions inside families.

- *Instruction without Encouragement:* Once again, as a coach I have been guilty of this one far too often. The desire to just drive, drive, drive and point out the path to improvement without ever stopping to praise or encourage can create a great deal of baggage in any child. We certainly are not perfect, so we shouldn't demand perfection from our children either.

- *Intrusions and Impositions:* Busy and stressed-out dads can get to the point where they see their children not as treasures but as life interruptions. Their constant questions and requests can become noise to us that interferes with everything from a business call to a TV show. Constantly feeling that "Dad thinks I'm just in the way" can wear a kid down until he or she feels worthless.

- *Pushing to Grow Up Too Fast:* Today's culture can easily usher kids straight from childhood into adulthood, skipping adolescence. Smartphones, technology, social media, and peer pressure bring children face-to-face with adult circumstances and issues far too soon and much too often. As dads, we have to work to counterbalance the culture by letting them be their age. Offer boundaries and parameters as expressions of love and security.

- *Overprotection:* The other side of the challenge in not pushing our children to grow up too fast is to avoid becoming what family counselors call a "helicopter parent." Such parents hover over their children constantly, smothering and not allowing conflict or consequences to occur so they can grow and mature.

Colossians 3:21 reminds us that an exasperated child can lose heart and give up trying to please a parent at all. What happens to any of us when we feel we can never measure up? We give up.

EVALUATING EXASPERATION

Next is a list of tough questions to examine and evaluate your parenting using the six "exasperators." Space is provided to write about any situations you need to address.

Where am I placing any unrealistic expectations on my kids?

Where am I comparing my kids to anyone else?

Where am I constantly instructing my kids with no encouragement?

Where am I treating my kids like they are intrusions and impositions?

Where am I pushing my kids to grow up too fast?

Where am I overprotecting and hovering over my kids?

As tough as this exercise may be for you, Dad, work hard to put yourself in your child's shoes. Evaluate your usual interactions with your kids. Think hard about your:

- words
- tone
- attitude
- voice volume level
- voice inflection
- negative facial expressions
- negative body language

Also avoid:

- hurtful sarcasm
- critical humor
- passive aggressiveness
- patronizing comments

These four negative methods of communication are unhealthy deflections of truth that we need to learn to communicate in the right way. For example, you see your child about to do something in a way you have attempted to correct several times, so you ask, "Oh, so you're going to try that your way one more time, huh?" The healthy question would be, "Before you try this time, remember what I have shown you before, okay?" How ironic that many parents are shocked when their kids become teenagers with a sarcastic attitude.

The reality is that we are constantly teaching our kids how to communicate both verbally and nonverbally. They will pick up our good and bad habits, doing what we do *and* what we say.

ENLISTING ENCOURAGEMENT

Now that we have covered the many ways we can discourage and exasperate our children, let's look at the great ways to encourage and speak life into them.

Be Authentic

One place we have to be certain where we are being our absolute and true best versions of ourselves is when we are with our kids. Because of their innocence, children can quickly sense a fake. They also know when we are being real with them.

In an age-appropriate way, explain to your children that each person has a spirit and flesh. Be honest with them that you, just like them, have a daily battle between your spirit (which wants to honor the Lord) and your flesh (which wants to serve yourself). We can give up pretending that we have to be perfect.

Your transparency could be the key to building a trusting relationship with them, and they will be encouraged that God is working on you in the places where you struggle as well.

Be Consistent

Consistency in our words and actions is such an important aspect of parenting. Jesus modeled consistency. He was the same man at the campfire that He was in the Temple, the same man with the woman at the well as with the Pharisee. He is our ultimate example.

One of the greatest gifts you can give your children is the security of them always knowing who you are going to be in any circumstance.

Admit Mistakes

Honest confession is crucial when we mess up in our families. We must model humility for our kids in both marriage and parenting. They need to see us stand up when we are right, but they also need to hear us 'fess up when we are wrong. Some of the most powerful and freeing words you can ever speak to your children are "Will you forgive me?"

Some of the most powerful and freeing words you can ever speak to your children are "Will you forgive me?"

Praise Often

Positively expressing to your kids how you feel about their victories is so important. But positively expressing how you feel about their failures—and their attempts to even try something—is also crucial. Placing your hand on each child and saying something positive to them every day is a great practice. Sow encouragement now, and you will reap by watching their courage later.

Express Joy

Life is stressful for most families today. Regardless of your personality or level of stress, remind yourself to show the love and joy of Christ to your kids. Laugh as often as you can. As Nehemiah said, "The joy of the LORD is your strength" (Neh. 8:10 NIV). Projecting joy as a dad on a daily basis is also a great way to balance those tough moments of discipline.

Give Grace

Paul's letters in Scripture consistently challenge us to be vessels of God's grace. Nowhere does offering grace apply more than inside our own families. Speak grace. Show grace.

Give Equal Treatment

Each child in a family is uniquely designed and skillfully created by God. Just as He doesn't show favoritism to His children, we cannot either with our kids (Rom. 2:11). Each child deserves his or her own unique relationship with you, while no child should have special treatment.

This may not apply when special needs are involved, but quantity necessary for one should warrant quality to the others.

Remember—oftentimes, the child you most butt heads with is the one most similar to you. That relationship can provide a mirror into how you need to change.

Speak into Your Child's God-Given Identity

No one knows your children better than you. While none of us may be experts on kids, we can become experts on *our* kids. As dads, we have the opportunity to speak God's identity into the hearts of our children. We must intentionally be louder, stronger, and more consistent than the many voices shouting at them in the world.

Take some time to write down each child's unique qualities, charac-
teristics, talents, skills, and spiritual gifts. Identify the fruits of the
Spirit from Galatians 5:22–23 that you see developing in your kids.
On a regular basis, speak those to your children. Pray those into their
lives as you pray for and over them. Find creative ways to remind
them of the amazing things God has placed into them.

One example would be to take your children's hands and have
them look at their fingerprints. Remind them that God made only
one set that looks like theirs. This provides proof that He made each
of their identities special. Like a master painter, He signed each one
of us as His one-of-a-kind masterpieces.

Let's dig deeper into this truth on identity by looking at the life
of Gideon in the Old Testament.

ME — *MIGHTY?*

The Israelites were being oppressed by a group of people called the
Midianites. At will, these enemies would invade the land and literally
take whatever they wanted. They killed any Israelite who got in their
way. When word would come of an approaching Midianite invasion,
the Israelites hid in caves in the mountains.

When we meet Gideon, he is threshing wheat. He's not outside
in the open, as was the custom, but inside a winepress. God sent
an angel to speak to him. As you read this passage, watch for how
Gideon clearly communicated how he felt about himself.

> The angel of the LORD came and sat down under
> the oak in Ophrah that belonged to Joash the
> Abiezrite, where his son Gideon was threshing

wheat in a winepress to keep it from the Midianites. When the angel of the LORD appeared to Gideon, he said, "The LORD is with you, mighty warrior."

"Pardon me, my lord," Gideon replied, "but if the LORD is with us, why has all this happened to us? Where are all his wonders that our ancestors told us about when they said, 'Did not the LORD bring us up out of Egypt?' But now the LORD has abandoned us and given us into the hand of Midian."

The LORD turned to him and said, "Go in the strength you have and save Israel out of Midian's hand. Am I not sending you?"

"Pardon me, my lord," Gideon replied, "but how can I save Israel? My clan is the weakest in Manasseh, and I am the least in my family."

The LORD answered, "I will be with you." (Judg. 6:11–16 NIV)

Like every Israelite, Gideon was scared to death of the Midianites. He hid in the winepress to thresh wheat for two reasons: out of fear of being found and to hide the wheat from the invaders. Typically, wheat was threshed outside on top of a hill so the wind would separate the grain from the chaff. Who would look for wheat where grapes were pressed?

Imagine Gideon's shock when this odd stranger suddenly appeared out of nowhere. The angel told him that the Lord was with him even though he was hiding like everyone else. The angel also told Gideon that God saw him as a mighty warrior. Both claims were apparently the last thing Gideon was thinking about himself.

When God called him a mighty warrior, Gideon was thinking, speaking, and acting like a coward. He described his clan as the weakest in the nation and himself as the least among them. One version of the Bible says that Gideon called himself "the runt of the litter" (Judg. 6:15 THE MESSAGE). What frame of mind do you have to be in to call yourself a runt?

But where Gideon saw only weakness, God could see a warrior. As his heavenly Father, God ignored Gideon's *feelings* to reveal the *fact* He knew was true about him.

Dad, let's apply this story to your life. Seeing yourself as Gideon is natural, but for this exercise, we're going to cast you as the angel and each of your children as Gideon. God has sent you to deliver a message from His lips to your children's hearts. Even when your kids feel weak, useless, unloved, and full of fear, you are God's designated representative, His messenger, sent to speak life into them. Now and as long as you live. What an amazing privilege as a dad!

God has sent you to deliver a message from His lips to your children's hearts.

One of my all-time favorite movies is *The Lion King*. The classic animated film tells a powerful story of a young lion cub named

Simba who comes to believe a lie and runs away to grow up denying his true identity. The turning point comes when his father, Mufasa, appears to him and says, "Simba, you are more than what you have become. You are the son of a king." Sound familiar? A little like Gideon maybe? What an incredible example of a father speaking life into his child.

Dad, we must keep telling our cubs who the Lion of Judah believes them to be. Regardless of circumstances or age, our kids need to hear from us that they are image-bearers of God, more than conquerors, and much-loved children of the King!

For many of us, parenting is the hardest, toughest, most challenging, and most complex role we will ever have. Right now, I hope you can hear your heavenly Father saying directly to you, "I am with you, mighty warrior!"

M46 Dads Challenge Eight

1. Plan an individual date night or outing with each of your kids. Take your child out for a special evening. It doesn't have to cost anything. What you do is up to you. During this dedicated and intentional time, tell your child the unique and special qualities you wrote out in the "God-given identity" teaching point in this chapter.

2. Speak life into your children before bedtime or before they leave for school by placing your hands on them and praying. Profess words of blessing and encouragement through your prayer.

3. The next time your child does something wrong or does anything he or she considers to be a failure, instead of dropping "the dad hammer," show grace and speak your child's true identity to him or her, just like God did for Gideon. In moments of your kid's weakness, speak warrior words.

Then the LORD said to Moses, "Tell Aaron and his sons to bless the people of Israel with this special blessing:

'May the LORD bless you
    and protect you.
May the LORD smile on you
    and be gracious to you.
May the LORD show you his favor
    and give you his peace.'" (Num. 6:22–26)

Fight for the hearts of your children!

Everett's M46 Moment

A Grandfather's Challenge

Although my children are all grown and I have grandchildren, I am still a father. So I never miss our M46 Dads CRASH. Every time I leave the meetings, I am amazed at how relevant the content is to us all. My only regret is that this ministry was not available when I was a young father—assuming I would have had the wisdom and devoted the time to take advantage of it back then.

In every CRASH meeting, the content is different but always so practical and necessary. Some might say it's too late for a grandfather or that there is too much water under the bridge. But that is just not true. While M46 Dads is about raising our children, the ministry is also about building lifelong relationships as a child of God, no matter your age, with other men to support and strengthen one another.

One of the greatest needs in our culture is for fathers to have a wholesome influence on their children. The rhino is truly a worthy symbol of that role. He is an undeniably huge presence, while not being invincible or immune to costly mistakes on his journey through the jungle.

Any self-respecting man *wants* to be a good father. We take whatever influence our father had on us and, by trial and error, work to improve our own parenting. If our dads had major shortcomings, we try to compensate. But because we too are sinners with failings and missed opportunities, our view and efforts are also flawed. The time when our children are at home goes by so fast. The M46 Dads movement can help us capture more of those years in a healthy way and allow for the opportunity for our children to prayerfully experience a better, richer life than we did.

The M46 Dads movement can allow for the opportunity for our children to prayerfully experience a better, richer life than we did.

The DNA of M46 Dads is different from anything I've experienced as a Christ-follower. The meetings are biblical, but they're not Bible studies. The time spent isn't "perfect dads" telling others what they should do and how they should parent. There is an openness and authenticity that welcomes *all* men who just want to be better dads, no matter their situation. The men who attend are broken, flawed, and imperfect. Just like me. But they are also Spirit-led to reach out and communicate in a way we can relate.

No matter our age, our children and grandchildren need us to fight for their hearts!

Part Three

FIELD

Chapter 9

The Battle Cry

Most dads who are also Christ-followers know we are in the midst of a spiritual battle with the powers of this world for the hearts of our children. Like it or not, then, accept it or not, we *are* God's warriors. If we don't fight for our children's hearts, who will?

Proverbs 29:18 states: "Where there is no vision, the people perish" (KJV). The New Living Translation is worded this way: "When people do not accept divine guidance, they run wild." In short, when we ignore God, we will run wild. Does that sound familiar in our current culture?

Fatherhood.org shares these stats about children growing up in a home with no dad:

- Four times greater risk of poverty
- Seven times greater risk of teen pregnancy
- Two times more likely to drop out of school

Other risks include behavioral problems, all forms of abuse and neglect, substance abuse, crime, prison, and even health issues like obesity. According to 2017 Census Bureau data, 19.7 million children have *no* father in the home—biological, step, or adopted. That is the obvious dark side.

But here's the upside when a dad *is* engaged in a child's life. An involved dad:

- improves a child's overall emotional and social well-being
- improves a child's performance in school
- reduces stress in family life
- reduces the chances a child will be mistreated *anywhere*[8]

Dads, while these facts show beyond any doubt that your direct involvement creates an offense *and* a defense for your family:

- Your offense gains new ground to increase opportunities for God's blessing and favor on your family.
- Your defense creates a protective barrier to diminish the chances for harm and hurt to get through to your family.

THE THREE *PS* OF AN M46 DAD

Your God-given role as a dad is vital to your family and sacred to your Father. How you choose to fulfill His plan impacts them and also the broader community where you live. Here are three of those primary roles you have as an M46 Dad:

1. Provider—you are called to do your best to provide for your family.

2. Protector—you are called to do your best to protect your family.

3. Priest—you are called to do your best to spiritually lead your family.

In the language of Proverbs 29:18, as a dad, you are to provide God's vision to your children because they desperately need stability and security as they grow and mature.

Most guys agree that God has called them to be financial providers and physical protectors of their families. But when we start talking about being the priest or the spiritual leader of the home, things can feel very intimidating. We don't feel equipped to do that, and we hate being asked to do things we don't know how to do.

When we start talking about being the priest or the spiritual leader of the home, things can feel very intimidating.

Many dads think, *Well, that's why we go to church. That's what my pastor is supposed to do.* Some guys pass the buck and say, "Oh, that's what my wife does, not me." Frankly, many men are simply terrified because we feel ill-equipped. We are quick to be proactive in so many areas of our lives, but in spiritual leadership, we can become passive to the point of being invisible in this one crucial responsibility.

Our culture teaches that wrong is right and right is wrong. So much evil is far too easily accessible to our children. They face dangerously real threats that can destroy them if we do not prepare them. Dad, we are shepherding God's sheep in a world of wolves. But the good news is that we are led by the Good Shepherd.

The bottom line is there are two plans available to our children: God's and the enemy's. Both have a strategy laid out for each child. Our kids will eventually choose one or the other as they start to navigate the world. While we cannot make the choices for our children, particularly as they get older, we can remain a major positive influence.

JOSHUA AT THE JORDAN

The story of Joshua offers dads strong doses of encouragement and challenge. This warrior chosen by God was given the huge responsibility of leading the Israelites in a conquest of the Promised Land, and the truths found in Joshua's story can help us become better equipped as the spiritual leaders of our homes.

Joshua was taking over the leadership mantle from Moses. The parting of the Red Sea and the rescue from Pharaoh's army were a tough act to follow. The first assignment given to Joshua was to lead the Israelites across the Jordan River. Doesn't sound so hard. But here's an important detail: the river was at flood stage.

Yet this time, there was no staff of Moses to hold high in the air and no waiting for the water to part. God told Joshua that when the people's feet touched the water, the river would divide. This was, of course, a huge test of faith in Joshua's leadership and also a new level of trust required from the people.

While Moses led the nation *away* from a threatening army, Joshua was being asked to lead the nation toward the enemy. On the other side of the Jordan, thirty-one hostile empires were *alerted and waiting* to destroy the Israelites.

Regardless of how unprepared and ill-equipped Joshua might have felt in the moment, God stepped in and gave the new leader some very specific counsel, peppered with promises. As you read the following passage, imagine that God is speaking these words to you:

> No one will be able to stand against you as long as you live. For I will be with you as I was with Moses. I will not fail you or abandon you.
>
> Be strong and courageous, for you are the one who will lead these people to possess all the land I swore to their ancestors I would give them. Be strong and very courageous. Be careful to obey all the instructions Moses gave you. Do not deviate from them, turning either to the right or to the left. Then you will be successful in everything you do. Study this Book of Instruction continually. Meditate on it day and night so you will be sure to obey everything written in it. Only then will you prosper and succeed in all you do. This is my command—be strong and courageous! Do not be afraid or discouraged. For the LORD your God is with you wherever you go. (Josh. 1:5–9)

How would you like to have God say that to you? Let's highlight the promises and directions found in these fourteen sentences:

1. No one will stand against you.
2. I will be with you.
3. I will not fail you.
4. I will not abandon you.
5. Be strong and courageous.
6. Be strong and *very* courageous.
7. Follow my instructions and you will be successful.
8. Follow my instructions and you will prosper and succeed.
9. Be strong and courageous.
10. Don't be afraid or discouraged.
11. God is with you—everywhere.

As a father, when you repeat something multiple times to your kids in one sitting, what is your goal? You are saying, "I want you to get this! Please! If you don't hear anything else, hear this." That was exactly what God was doing by repeating this message to Joshua—and to us.

Dad, Joshua's story is *your* story. You are the warrior-leader. Your wife and kids are the Israelites. The Jordan River is your everyday life. The opposing armies are the many types of evil coming at your family. But here's the best part: you and Joshua have the *same* God leading you! The same God who made those promises to Joshua offers them to you today in whatever circumstances you face as a father.

The same God who made those promises to Joshua offers them to you today in whatever circumstances you face as a father.

Like Joshua with Israel, we dads have a huge responsibility to lead our families. Life, like the crossing of the Jordan, is going to have some terrifying moments. We are going to be discouraged and afraid at times. There will even be seasons that make us feel that we are being attacked from thirty-one directions. But the same powerful promises are available to each of us.

FINDING YOUR STRENGTH AND COURAGE

Crafted into God's speech to Joshua is a Hebrew battle cry: *"Rak Chazak Amats!"* This phrase translates as "only be strong and courageous."

- Rak—do only what follows
- Chazak—be strong; act like a man
- Amats—take courage; make secure[9]

Diving a little deeper into the Hebrew word *amats* (pronounced "aw-mats"), here is a more detailed version of its definition:

- Strong, brave, bold
- To strengthen, secure, make firm, make obstinate, assure
- To be determined, to make oneself alert, persist in[10]

If a man is brave, bold, secure, assured, determined, and alert, he is displaying a proactive courage.

But the truth is that most of us dads don't think of ourselves as having supernatural strength or courage. Sometimes we feel like saying, "I'm sick and tired of fighting for my family. I'm worn out. I *am* discouraged. I *am* afraid. In fact, I'm just done." Or we can become complacent and begin to drift away from God and our responsibility to our families.

Regardless, the absolutely essential truth for us to understand and receive is that our Rak Chazak Amats—our true strength and courage—cannot and will not come from ourselves but from God. The game changer for Joshua was the many times God repeated, "Don't be afraid. I will be with you." God's presence resides in His power, and it is the only path to victory, then and now.

A great temptation with which we all struggle is to fight out of our own strength, completely motivated and influenced by our flesh. But no matter how strong we are or think we are, our flesh will wear out. We find out quickly that our bodies are not strong enough, our minds are not smart enough, and our wills are not disciplined enough.

If we all jumped into the Pacific Ocean to see who could swim to Hawaii, some of us would make it farther than others, but no one would arrive on the coast of the Big Island. Even in an effort to be a selfless dad and husband, we can only get so far in our own strength.

In a previous chapter, we talked about the Temple of God now being inside us as Christ-followers. His Spirit is placed inside us. Therefore, where does our strength and courage come from? The answer: Christ, who is in us. Our identity in Him is our only eternal source of heavenly boldness.

Knowing God's specific will for all the many aspects of our lives can often be difficult and challenging to grasp and understand. But finding God's desire for us as fathers has been made perfectly clear in Scripture as He commands each of us to:

1. Teach your children

> And you must commit yourselves wholeheartedly to these commands that I am giving you today. Repeat them again and again to your children. Talk about them when you are at home and when you are on the road, when you are going to bed and when you are getting up. (Deut. 6:6–7)

2. Discipline your children

> Fathers, do not provoke your children to anger by the way you treat them. Rather, bring them up with the discipline and instruction that comes from the Lord. (Eph. 6:4)

3. Guide your children

> The godly walk with integrity; blessed are their children who follow them. (Prov. 20:7)

4. Love your children

> Love is patient and kind. Love is not jealous or boastful or proud or rude. It does not demand its own way. It is not irritable, and it keeps no record of being wronged. It does not rejoice about injustice but rejoices whenever the truth wins out. Love never gives up, never loses faith, is always hopeful, and endures through every circumstance. (1 Cor. 13:4–7)

5. Serve with your children

> So fear the LORD and serve him wholeheartedly.... But as for me and my family, we will serve the LORD. (Josh. 24:14–15)

6. Protect your children

> Those who respect the LORD will have security, and their children will be protected. (Prov. 14:26 NCV)

7. Be proud of your children

> Children are a gift from the LORD;
>   they are a reward from him.
> Children born to a young man
>   are like arrows in a warrior's hands.
> How joyful is the man whose quiver is full of them!
>   (Ps. 127:3–5)

8. Leave a legacy for your children

> The good man's children will be powerful in the
>   land;
>   his descendants will be blessed. (Ps. 112:2 GNT)

9. Pray for your children

> Pour out your hearts like water to the Lord.
> Lift up your hands to him in prayer,
>   pleading for your children. (Lam. 2:19)

10. Have compassion for your children

> As a father has compassion on his children,
>   so the LORD has compassion on those who fear
>   him. (Ps. 103:13 NIV)

And of course, all ten declarations point back to our ministry theme verse of Malachi 4:6 to turn your heart toward your children.

Just as God's desire and will were clearly for Joshua to lead the Israelites, His heart is for you to be the priest of your own home, the spiritual leader for your family. You can have the bold confidence that He is with you as you fight for their hearts.

Dad, we challenge you to embrace this Hebrew war cry as your own—"Rak Chazak Amats!" As you face times of hardship and challenge, pray, "God, I thank You that You are with me, just like You were with Joshua. Strengthen me in Your name. Give me Your courage."

STAND STRONG, STEP UP, STEP OUT

Looking back a few verses, we see that God made this promise to Joshua: "Wherever you set foot, you will be on land I have given you" (Josh. 1:3). God was most certainly with Joshua.

But notice that God would give Joshua only the land where he set foot. He couldn't sit in his tent and wait for God to act. The warrior-leader still had to take that divine strength and courage, choose to step out, and intentionally engage in the battle.

The same principle is true with you and your family in the midst of your own daily battle. Whether you feel like you are on offense, moving forward to your "new land," or on defense, just trying to hold your ground, God wants to give you greater influence in the lives of your children, for their good and His glory.

While we can all feel inadequate and ill-equipped to be the priests of our own homes, we must be obedient and choose to be God's man for our families. Then He will take care of the rest. Like the

Jordan River, which would begin to dry up only when the people's feet touched the water, or like Joshua, who conquered new ground with every footstep forward, God is with you, priest of the Lord. No matter what you have done in the past, He promises to equip and empower you to be His leader in your home.

We began this chapter with some disturbing stats about homes with no dads. Let's close with some words of biblical empowerment as you commit to be a strong and courageous M46 Dad:

- God has given you His Spirit.
- God has given you a mission.
- God is with you to fight your battle.
- The days of being passive are behind you.
- You can step out in faith for your family.
- You can step up and lead to give vision to your family.
- God gave you children, so He believes in you as a father to lead them in His name.
- God has given you a battle cry.

Dad, be strong and courageous. He is with you as you fight for the hearts of your children. *Rak Chazak Amats!*

> And you are living stones that God is building into his spiritual temple. What's more, you are his holy priests. Through the mediation of Jesus Christ, you offer spiritual sacrifices that please God. As the Scriptures say,

"I am placing a cornerstone in Jerusalem,
    chosen for great honor,
and anyone who trusts in him
    will never be disgraced."

Yes, you who trust him recognize the honor
God has given him … for you are a chosen people.
You are royal priests, a holy nation, God's very
own possession. As a result, you can show others
the goodness of God, for he called you out of the
darkness into his wonderful light. (1 Pet. 2:5–7, 9)

M46 Dads Challenge Nine

One way to model Christlike servant leadership and priesthood to your children, while also setting your family's feet on new ground, is to volunteer to minister together. Lead them in service as a team. Depending on the age of your children, here are a few suggestions of places where you might serve:

- children's hospital
- nursing home
- food pantry
- homeless shelter
- offer childcare for a single mom
- repair work for an elderly widow

Embrace your role as the physical protector, financial provider, and priest (the spiritual leader) of your family. God is with you as you fight for the hearts of your children.

> Then the King will say to those on his right, "Come, you who are blessed by my Father, inherit the Kingdom prepared for you from the creation of the world. For I was hungry, and you fed me. I was thirsty, and you gave me a drink. I was a stranger, and you invited me into your home. I was naked, and you gave me clothing. I was sick, and you cared for me. I was in prison, and you visited me."

Then these righteous ones will reply, "Lord, when did we ever see you hungry and feed you? Or thirsty and give you something to drink? Or a stranger and show you hospitality? Or naked and give you clothing? When did we ever see you sick or in prison and visit you?"

And the King will say, "I tell you the truth, when you did it to one of the least of these my brothers and sisters, you were doing it to me!" (Matt. 25:34–40)

Fight for the hearts of your children!

Drew's M46 Moment

Live Every Day for What Matters

I was your typical Christian guy. I loved God and my family. I was also a healthy man in my forties. Or I thought I was healthy.

One day, I went from feeling great to feeling awful. Just two days later, I was lying in a hospital bed fighting for my life. Yes, I was literally on my deathbed.

Not knowing if I would live or die, I had the most difficult conversation with my wife that we had ever had. I explained to her what she would need to do financially and told her how much I loved her. I told my son that if I didn't make it, he would have to become the man of the house and take care of his mom for me. I told him how proud I was to have him as my son. I realized in that moment that it feels almost impossible to accurately express to your family how much you really love them.

The doctor's tests revealed that I have a "factor five" blood condition that makes me more prone to blood clots. Apparently, the clot that was threatening my life had been there for several years. But instead of breaking apart and going up into my lungs or heart, which would have killed me, the clot had gone down into my leg. That was quite unusual, the doctors told me. Blood clots normally travel toward your heart, not away.

When I heard that, I knew God was trying to get my attention.

Lying there, helpless, I realized that my Father had given me a second chance to get my life right. I had been fully focused on my business and had lost sight of what truly matters in life. My thoughts were very simple: I had forgotten the true meaning of life—faith and family come before *anything*.

Lying there, helpless, I realized that my Father had given me a second chance to get my life right.

But God answered our prayers to bring healing, and the treatment worked. I recovered and was released to a fresh start. He used this close call to remind me of the truth, and I vowed to never forget again.

Today, I actually feel fortunate that this crisis occurred in my life, which brought me closer to God and my family. I work to show them every day how much I love them. I have a sign that reminds me: "Live every day for what matters!"

A major challenge in M46 Dads is to reorder your life around what really matters. I actually lived that, and I have shared my testimony with other men. My situation was not a hypothetical fast-forward to my distant deathbed. For me, it was very real. All that mattered on that day was my relationship with my Father, my relationship with my Family, and my relationships, my impact, on my Field. The greatest life lesson we can learn as men who follow Christ is to know at the end of life all that matters is God and our families!

Chapter 10

Becoming a Reconciling Rhino

As we head into our final chapter, let's do a quick review of one of our key foundational truths in the M46 Dad experience.

The pursuit of religion is:

- fear-based
- behavior-focused
- performance-driven

In the pursuit of religion:

- law overshadows grace
- condemnation overrides conviction
- accusation overpowers acceptance

For too long in the Western church, we have seen what a mess this man-made paradigm makes. Just look again at those statistics of fatherless homes.

That's the bad news. Now here's the good news. Being truly transformed by the gospel of Christ allows our kids to see Jesus in us. They get to see what He "looks like" in their dad. Seeing and experiencing Him through your life will more likely draw them into their own relationships with Jesus.

There's an old adage that says "God doesn't have any grand-children." No one inherits salvation or "grandfathers" into heaven. Each person has a will and therefore has to have his or her own encounter and journey with God. Your kids will eventually need to have their own faith and their own personal experiences with Jesus.

Christ knew what the teachers of the law were lording over the people, and He wanted to present the truth that He came to offer.

> Come to me, all you who are weary and burdened,
> and I will give you rest. Take my yoke upon you
> and learn from me, for I am gentle and humble
> in heart, and you will find rest for your souls. For
> my yoke is easy and my burden is light. (Matt.
> 11:28–30 NIV)

As the perfect Father, God wants His kids to be motivated by love *for* Him, not fear *of* Him. So we also want our kids' lives to be driven by love, not fear.

> By this is love perfected with us, so that we may
> have confidence for the day of judgment, because
> as he is so also are we in this world. There is no fear

in love, but perfect love casts out fear. For fear has
to do with punishment, and whoever fears has not
been perfected in love. We love because he first
loved us. (1 John 4:17–19 ESV)

FUELING THE FIRES OF FAITH

Dad, you have to *gather up* spiritual kindling today for the fire of
your children's faith if you want them to *grow up* to know God and
love Him. You can then pray that He fuels their fire to burn strong
for the rest of their lives. Anything you attempt to light for them in
your own power will not last. A true spiritual fire is one that God
has *manifested*, not one you have *manipulated*.

So what is this spiritual kindling that we can gather for our
children today?

First, we would all agree that the fundamentals of faith—such as
prayer, Bible study, church attendance, and Christian community—
are necessary elements for consistent spiritual growth. These are the
spiritual disciplines that we all need to engage in and practice.

But the generations being raised up today have far higher expectations and demands for a spiritual experience than ours and past
generations. From the younger side of Millennials and including
all of Gen Z, research shows the thirty-and-under crowd needs to
see the gospel at work to believe. Better yet, they need to *experience* it to believe. They don't and won't accept anyone's "just because
you're supposed to" efforts to guide them to faith. They don't ask just
"What?" but also "Why?"

Josh Chen, the missions director for CRU, explained this concept well in an interview with Barna Research:

> For Millennials and Gen Z, the good news of
> the gospel is that salvation is not only for later,
> it is something that is happening now—without
> diminishing the importance of "later." Jesus wants
> us to experience wholeness now—physically,
> spiritually, emotionally and relationally. So when
> it comes to their felt needs, we need to offer young
> people more than just platitudes or future prom-
> ises. We need to walk them through the hard work
> of spiritual formation and an invitation to experi-
> ence the power of the Holy Spirit. Right now.[11]

There is clear evidence that our kids will not be satisfied just faking faith, as many in previous generations did. They want the gospel in real time in real life. At M46 Dads, we believe that is a very good thing. So, in light of this need, let's talk about one powerful piece of kindling we need to gather for God's fire to make a major impact in the lives of our children. This is a countercultural aspect of the gospel that we too must believe and receive.

Have you ever wondered why, once God has saved us, He leaves us here to live for a time? Why doesn't He just take us on to our home in heaven? Is the purpose only so we can lead a happier life on the other side of salvation? Of course not. We all quickly discover that the Christian walk doesn't guarantee the absence of trials and pain in our lives. For some, their surrender to Jesus actually makes life tougher because of hard choices they must make.

So why are we still here?

RUNNING INTO THE FIRE

We have all seen the news footage of massive fires where everyone is running out of a burning building. We see the firefighters and rescue squads storming into the inferno. In recent years, we have seen clips from cameras attached to Marines' helmets as they rushed into a chaotic scene beneath the constant barrage of automatic weapon fire.

The same scene plays out with police: While everyone is fleeing a shooting, officers are heading toward the bullets. While people are sheltered at home to escape a pandemic, ER doctors and nurses go in to help and heal, risking their very lives.

All first responders take this action. In fact, that is their title— first to respond. This commitment is always very moving when we see the selflessness and bravery of what these everyday heroes do, stirring up powerful inspiration every time.

There is no doubt that these individuals are heroes. But how does God define a hero? What does He count as brave and bold?

To God, a hero is someone who walks into someone else's mess to minister in His name. Someone who shows compassion and empathy toward the people whom everyone else rejects. Someone who cares for those who are invisible to everyone else. Someone who commits to "be Jesus" to the world, even to the people who have "set their own fires."

To be a first responder, you must meet certain age, health, and physical criteria. But in the kingdom of God, a first grader who takes up for a friend while the other kids make fun of him is a hero. An elderly person who listens to and prays for a hurting neighbor is a hero. Someone with special needs who cannot speak but gives constant hugs with a smile is a hero.

Why are Christians still here? In the following passage, Paul gives us a strong message as to our purpose on this earth between salvation and heaven, as well as how to be a hero in God's kingdom:

> Therefore, if anyone is in Christ, the new creation has come: The old has gone, the new is here! All this is from God, who reconciled us to himself through Christ and gave us the ministry of reconciliation: that God was reconciling the world to himself in Christ, not counting people's sins against them. And he has committed to us the message of reconciliation. We are therefore Christ's ambassadors, as though God were making his appeal through us. We implore you on Christ's behalf: Be reconciled to God. God made him who had no sin to be sin for us, so that in him we might become the righteousness of God. (2 Cor. 5:17–21 NIV)

We're here to serve as Christ's ambassadors, bringing His kingdom to our culture.

If the government appoints you as an ambassador to another country, you don't go there to communicate your own messages and do your own will. You are called to speak on behalf of the leader who sent you to carry out his plan and purposes. You are merely a representative of the leader, not a free agent representing yourself. The vast majority of your role is to keep peace and maintain good relations between your nation and the host nation.

Being appointed ambassador is a great honor. Look at these phrases from the passage: "committed to us the message," "making his appeal through us," and "on Christ's behalf." The only way we can authentically and accurately carry out God's plan and purpose is to live in a relationship with Him through Christ. If we want to accurately convey His words and will, we'd better be listening to His messages. Then we have to share, verbalize, and exemplify His gospel.

God has clearly appointed you as His ambassador to represent Him to your culture and in all your circles of influence. Your purpose, your job, is to conduct the ministry of showing and telling others that He wants to reconcile with them.

> For God so loved the world, that he gave his only Son, that whoever believes in him should not perish but have eternal life. For God did not send his Son into the world to condemn the world, but in order that the world might be saved through him. (John 3:16–17 ESV)

As an M46 Dad, your kids need to see you are not ashamed to tell people about Jesus and to show people the love of Jesus.

We are now living in a post-Christian society. The Bible's truths and the ways of God are no longer held as the standard by the general population. Even in the church, many adhere to the ever-changing cries of culture over the Word of God. The methods we used to communicate the gospel even twenty years ago rarely work today.

But while we have to *customize the method* to share Christ, we must never *compromise the message*.

But while we have to *customize the method* to share Christ, we must never *compromise the message*.

We have to look for opportunities to have gospel conversations with people as we encounter them in the marketplace, community, and neighborhood. If Jesus is a real part of who we are, then He can naturally be brought up as we talk about life. Also, asking people the right questions about their lives can be a compelling way to introduce Christ.

FAITH RESPONDERS

We see in the life of Jesus how important relationships are to God. When Jesus returned from the desert to begin His ministry, He didn't walk down the shoreline and form an army. He didn't build a stage, showcase His gifts, or raise money for a new temple to speak at once a week.

Rather, Jesus called men one by one. He gathered a small group of rough-around-the-edges guys who would huddle around a campfire with Him at night. Jesus chose people He could pour into, not those who thought they were already full. He constantly ignored the racism and biases of the day to talk with women, children, the poor, foreigners, broken sinners, heathen, outcasts, and "the least of these."

Jesus earned the right to teach the people about the kingdom of God by ministering and meeting needs before He preached the kingdom of God. He walked with them to win the right to talk to them. We are His ambassadors, so we must do things His way. We are to demonstrate the love and grace of God to broken and hurting people—those outside *and* inside the church.

The strange thing about Churchworld is that we can be awesome when someone has a death in the family, is diagnosed with cancer, or gets into an accident. We will love on those people, care for them, take food to their houses, and even help financially. But what do we do when people are responsible for bringing harm into their own lives? We can too quickly adopt the attitude of "Well, they made their bed, so now they have to lie in it." And then there are the Scripture-quoters who say, "See? You reap what you sow."

But whether they are hurt by no fault of their own or because they sinned intentionally by their own hand, we can be like Jesus and run toward broken and messy people. When someone's marriage is falling apart, or when a man ends up in jail or makes some life-altering mistake, we can be like first responders. We can teach our kids to be *faith responders*. Teach them how to be ministers of reconciliation in the lives of the people in their circles of influence.

Christ-followers cannot treat broken and hurting people like victims of a car wreck on the side of the road. We can't just slow down, take a look, and then hit the gas to go back to normal life. We are called to be the heart, hands, and feet of Jesus to minister and share the gospel. We have been given the ministry of reconciliation.

But we must also match our *will to help* with the *wisdom to hear*. In my years of ministry, I have had to weigh my deep compassion for people's apparent difficult circumstances with the tough questions of how and why they got where they are. I have had to learn to ask, what do they truly need? Our balance in wisdom and perspective will come only through the Holy Spirit's guidance in each circumstance. Jesus continually modeled that level of obedience.

One such example is in John 8, the story of the woman caught in the act of adultery. The teachers of the law brought her before Christ with the intent to trap Him on a technicality and then stone her.

Jesus' response was to encourage anyone who had *not* sinned to cast the first stone at her. The ironic truth about His words was that He was the only person there who could actually throw a stone. The men quietly dropped their rocks, along with their accusations, and left. Jesus also encouraged the woman to go in freedom but to change her life.

Paul urges us like this: "Brothers, if anyone is caught in any transgression, you who are spiritual should restore him in a spirit of gentleness. Keep watch on yourself, lest you too be tempted" (Gal. 6:1 ESV).

The word *caught* in this verse means "like in a spider web or net, trapped and not able to shake loose." *You who are spiritual* refers to those who walk daily with God and are capable of helping hurting people. This does not authorize anyone to throw stones. The implication of Paul's words is that if you are not spiritual, then you should keep out of the situation. That was why he went on to encourage them to "restore that person gently."

For many years, the sentence "Keep watch on yourself, lest you too be tempted" has been understood to mean something like "Don't go in a bar and talk to a filthy alcoholic or you might end up getting drunk yourself." That is an incorrect interpretation designed to rationalize letting ourselves off the hook so we don't have to get into messy ministry. The sentence actually means "Don't judge too harshly and think you're above falling into a pit yourself."

> Confess your sins to each other and pray for each other so that you may be healed. The earnest prayer of a righteous person has great power and produces wonderful results.... My dear brothers and sisters, if someone among you wanders away from the truth and is brought back, you can be sure that whoever brings the sinner back from wandering will save that person from death and bring about the forgiveness of many sins. (James 5:16, 19–20)

How many people have had a moral failure, felt judged, been outcast, then just drifted away from the church, and eventually from God, never wanting anything to do with faith again? They wandered too far, were rejected too harshly, and became too discouraged. Sometimes we find ourselves acting like Joshua in one season of our lives but Gideon—or even Judas—in another. "Strong and courageous" can become "despair and discouragement" without the right help.

Sometimes we find ourselves acting like Joshua in one season of our lives but Gideon—or even Judas—in another.

RADICAL RESCUE

Our good friend Mark Hall, of the Christian band Casting Crowns, shared a story he heard from a man who had led a US Special Forces combat unit. On one particular mission, they had to go in and rescue a group of people somewhere in the Middle East. After taking out the guards, they found the room where the captives were being held.

The soldier called out, "Hey, we're Americans. We're here to take you home." But no one moved. They just lay there. So he said again, louder, "Hey! We're Americans. We've come to take you home. You're safe now." Still they would not move.

What the Special Forces soldiers did not yet know was their captors had often run into the room and said, "The Americans are here to rescue you. Come on. Come outside." But every time they ran out, they were all severely beaten, kicked, and thrown back into the room. They had become so conditioned and fearful that they wouldn't move even to go to the bathroom. With broken spirits and no hope of rescue, they had been living in their own filth.

Being trained in the psychological tactics of terrorists, the soldiers finally realized what had happened. The soldier told Mark, "I couldn't get them to believe me … that they were safe … that we were there to rescue them. So I took off some of my gear and walked over to where they were. I laid down next to them, right there in their filth." Gently, calmly, I told them again, 'We're Americans, and we're here to take you home with us.' Slowly, one by one, they got up and walked out to freedom."

He finished his story: "I had to get down in the filth *with them* before they would believe anything I said *to them*."

The radical love and grace of Jesus drove Him to come *to us* to live in our filth *with us* so He could *rescue us*.

Dad, let your kids see you being:

- an ambassador for Christ by speaking His message
- a minister of reconciliation by sharing His mercy

The age-old quote of St. Francis "Preach the gospel everywhere, and if necessary, use words" was never intended to be an excuse not to share verbally. Rather, we are to be so proactive in ministry that by the time you tell your children the gospel, they are ready because they have seen its power alive in your life.

Let your kids see Jesus in you by what you do for others. Let the reflection of their heavenly Father shine through the heart, words, and actions of their earthly father. That is what being an M46 Dad is all about.

M46 Dads Challenge Ten

Our final challenge is in two parts:

1. Your Testimony

Your testimony is simply your story of how Christ brought you to Himself by His Spirit. No matter the details, your salvation is miraculous and unique in its own way. People can debate and question you on the Bible and spiritual truths, but no one can argue with your changed heart. Your story is His-story!

Here is a very simple way to talk about your faith in a gospel conversation—your own story of what the Lord has done for you. In three to four sentences for each point, write down the ending of each sentence prompt:

My life before Christ was:

I came to know Christ by/through:

My relationship with Jesus changed my life by:

Today, God is at work in my life by/through:

After you write out your testimony, go over it and memorize your story enough to be able to quickly and concisely share your faith with anyone. Practice on your kids.

> Always be prepared to give an answer to everyone
> who asks you to give the reason for the hope that
> you have. But do this with gentleness and respect.
> (1 Pet. 3:15 NIV)

2. Your Ministry

Take a few minutes away from distractions to prayerfully make a list of "the least of these" in your life, those people whom others are running away from, those people who need to see the love of Jesus in you. Pray for an opportunity, and seek out a gospel conversation with them.

Finally, depending on the age of your kids, how can you involve them in your ministry and teach them about ministry? How can you inspire and challenge them to do the same in their circles at school, in the neighborhood, at church, and with friends online?

A great conversation to have with them is how to use social media to glorify God and minister to others. Talk honestly about the issues raised by being online and how they can choose to be a part of the solution and not add to the problem.

Allow God to first use you as an ambassador of Christ and a minister of reconciliation. Then teach your children how to do the same in all their circles.

> In the same way, let your light shine before others,
> so that they may see your good works and give glory
> to your Father who is in heaven. (Matt. 5:16 ESV)

Statistics tell us that 88 percent of children who grow up in evangelical churches will leave the faith after graduating high school. But when a child grows up in a home where the father and mother have been actively modeling their faith and are engaged in ministering to people, that number drops to as low as 5 percent.[12]

You want your kids to know and love God? Show them what He's like!

Fight for the hearts of your children!

Your M46 Moment

Fighting for the Hearts of Your Kids

You have read our stories and the stories of several dads like you. Before you move to the final section of this book, we have an important question for you: What is *your* M46 Moment?

What M46 story would you submit to us? Or maybe you're looking forward to and praying for yours to come soon as you have completed this book and the challenges.

In the space below, write your story. God wants to add your M46 Moment to ours as you walk alongside Him to be the spiritual leader in your home.

Charge Forward

Congratulations on completing *Fight for Their Hearts*! Our hope and prayer have been that you will continue to:

1. submit to Christ's transformational work in your life
2. commit to being intentional in your children's lives

This fatherhood business is not as easy as it's sometimes made out to be. If there's a manual that comes with the first baby, somehow we missed it. We don't feel like we're exactly crushing it in our own lives very often, so how are we supposed to teach children how to do it well?

But it does help to get focused on the things that matter most, the things we want said about us at our funerals. Father, Family, and Field help condense the problem down. And it really helps to know that God calls us to and provides Rak Chazak Amats, our true strength and courage.

God's word to Joshua is for us too: "This is my command—be strong and courageous! Do not be afraid or discouraged. For the LORD your God is with you wherever you go" (Josh. 1:9).

Maybe you had a great role model for a father figure, and maybe you didn't. But you loom large in your kids' lives, like a massive rhino, and no one can be that person for them for you. You've answered the bell and the call to battle, and you're ready to do what God calls you to, including showing your faults and uncertainty, to turn your heart to your kids and their hearts to you.

WHAT'S NEXT?

We hope that *Fight for Their Hearts* has been an amazing start to, or continuation of, your journey of living with your heart turned to your kids.

But this material has been developed for use in a group. This road is a hard one, and few things help more on a road like that than someone to travel it with. We created M46 to be like AA for dads, which means we have always done it in groups, where dads can find support, humor, and encouragement from others on the same path. *Fight for Their Hearts* has been your introduction, but where M46 really comes into its own is in the CRASH communities.

Now that you're committed to this course, it's time to find (or create) a CRASH community where you and others like you can compare notes, share parenting war stories, and get put back on your feet.

At these CRASHes, you'll watch the videos that we have prepared for you. There's nothing like watching these with other dads and then talking about them together. There's no substitute for hearing how others around the table have fallen on their butts even worse than you did in their first attempts at doing one of the challenges. Our society likes to keep us hidden away in our own barricaded homes, but the truth is that you have fellow warriors with you in the battle, and you need them. And they need you.

Here's your action plan:

- Go to **www.M46Dads.com** to learn more about the ministry.
- Find a local CRASH near you. Learn where and when they meet. Write it on your calendar, and commit to going to their next meeting.
- If there isn't one near you, commit to launching one with some other dads you know, even if it's just one or two total and even if you have to meet online. Getting the thing started is more important than doing it "big." Big can happen later.
- To prepare you to run your own CRASH, we have developed a leader-training process, which you can learn more about on the site. As a bonus on top of the training, you can download the free *M46 Crash Course Leader's Guide* that you'll find on the site.
- Order one or more copies of the *M46 Crash Course Participant's Guide*, which will be your workbooks for the CRASH sessions.
- Go to or host the next CRASH.

You are mighty, fellow dad, in the sense that you are a massive presence in the lives of your children, and God lives in you. But it's important to acknowledge that as fathers we are in desperate need

of God's help, and the help of our brothers in Christ. You are irre-
placeable in your children's hearts. But you're also not all-powerful
or all-knowing. You need the help of other dads and the guidance we
provide in the videos, and you need prayer.

In short, you need a CRASH community and the *M46 Crash
Course Participant's Guide*. They've been designed from the ground
up to support you in this great cause of turning the hearts of the children to their fathers and the hearts of the fathers to their children.

Rak Chazak Amats! Be strong and courageous!

Notes

1. Larry Taylor, *Running with the Horses: A Parenting Guide for Raising Children to Be Servant-Leaders for Christ* (Nashville: Westbow Press, 2013), 33.

2. Merriam-Webster Online Dictionary, s.v. "revolution," accessed December 7, 2020, www.merriam-webster.com/dictionary/revolution.

3. Alina Bradford, "Facts about Rhinos," Live Science, March 20, 2018, www.livescience.com/27439-rhinos.html.

4. Luke Ward, "20 Fascinating Facts about Rhinos That You Should Know," The Fact Site, accessed April 15, 2020, www.thefactsite.com/rhino-facts/.

5. Ward, "20 Fascinating Facts."

6. Merriam-Webster Online Dictionary, s.v. "hypocrite," accessed December 7, 2020, www.merriam-webster.com/dictionary/hypocrite.

7. John Ericson, "Incredible Self-Surgeries in History," Medical Daily, August 27, 2013, www.medicaldaily.com/incredible-self-surgeries-history-do-it-yourself -procedures-include-appendectomy-amputation-254751.

8. "The Proof Is In: Father Absence Harms Children," National Fatherhood Initiative, 2017, accessed December 7, 2020, www.fatherhood.org/fatherhood -data-statistics.

9. "Joshua's War Cry," Day 1, Bible.com, accessed December 7, 2020, www.bible .com/reading-plans/17949-joshua-warcry/day/1.

10. NAS Old Testament Hebrew Lexicon, s.v. "amats," BibleStudyTools.com, accessed December 7, 2020, www.biblestudytools.com/lexicons/hebrew/nas/amats .html.

11. David Kinnaman, Roxy Lee Stone, and Brooke Hempell, "Josh Chen on the Spiritual Curiosity of Young People," Barna Group, May 28, 2019, www.barna .com/josh-chen-millennials-gen-z/.

12. Jerry Pipes and Victor Lee, *Family to Family: Leaving a Lasting Legacy* (Alpharetta, GA: North American Mission Board of the Southern Baptist Convention, 1999), 50.

Bible Credits

Unless otherwise noted, all Scripture quotations are taken from the *Holy Bible*, New Living Translation, copyright © 1996, 2015 by Tyndale House Foundation. Used by permission of Tyndale House Publishers, Inc., Carol Stream, Illinois 60188. All rights reserved.

Scripture quotations marked ASV are taken from the American Standard Version. (Public Domain.)

Scripture quotations marked ESV are taken from the ESV® Bible (The Holy Bible, English Standard Version®), copyright © 2001 by Crossway, a publishing ministry of Good News Publishers. Used by permission. All rights reserved.

Scripture quotations marked GNT are taken from the Good News Translation in Today's English Version—Second Edition. Copyright © 1992 by American Bible Society. Used by permission.

Scripture quotations marked GW are taken from the GOD'S WORD Translation. Copyright © 1995, 2020 by God's Word to the Nations Mission Society. All rights reserved.

Scripture quotations marked KJV are taken from the King James Version. (Public Domain.)

Scripture quotations marked THE MESSAGE are taken from THE MESSAGE. Copyright © by Eugene H. Peterson 1993, 2018. Used by permission of Tyndale House Publishers, Inc.

Scripture quotations marked NASB are taken from the New American Standard Bible®, copyright © 1960, 1995, 2020 by The Lockman Foundation. Used by permission. (www.Lockman.org.)

Scripture quotations marked NCV are taken from the New Century Version®. Copyright © 2005 by Thomas Nelson. Used by permission. All rights reserved.

Scripture quotations marked NIV are taken from THE HOLY BIBLE, NEW INTERNATIONAL VERSION®, NIV® Copyright © 1973, 2011 by Biblica, Inc.® Used by permission. All rights reserved worldwide.

Scripture quotations marked NLV are taken from the Holy Bible, New Life Version. Copyright © 1969–2003 by Christian Literature International, P.O. Box 777, Canby, OR 97013. Used by permission.

The authors have added italics to Scripture quotations for emphasis.